The Second Coming of Christ

By

Rev. Clarence Larkin
author of the great book
"DISPENSATIONAL TRUTH"

Published by the

REV. CLARENCE LARKIN ESTATE
P. O. Box 334, Glenside, Pa. 19038
U.S.A.

THE ASCENSION

"This SAME JESUS, which is taken up from you into Heaven shall so come IN LIKE MANNER as ye have seen Him GO INTO HEAVEN." Acts 1:11.

Foreword

Having been solicited on numerous occasions by friends who love the

"BLESSED HOPE"

to prepare a small comprehensive pamphlet on the

SECOND COMING OF CHRIST

illustrated with a few simple charts for the information of those who may desire to know about the Lord's Return, the Author has prepared this little booklet and sends it forth on its mission praying that God will richly bless its testimony.

THE AUTHOR.

"SUNNYSIDE," Fox Chase, Phila., Pa.
October 28, 1918

Contents

SUBJECTS

CHARTS AND ILLUSTRATIONS

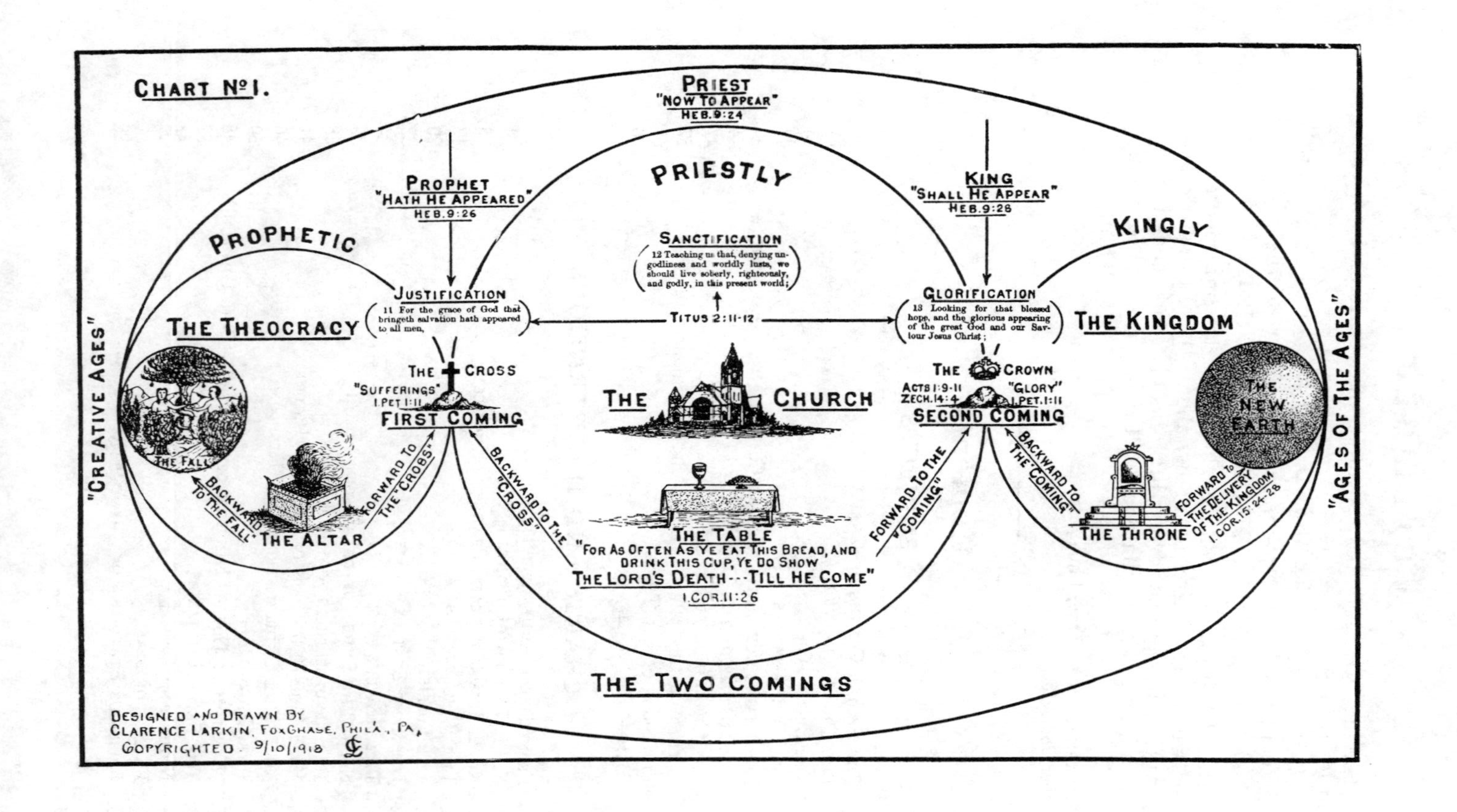

CHART No 1.
PRIEST
"NOW TO APPEAR"
HEB.9:24
PRIESTLY
PROPHET
"HATH HE APPEARED"
HEB.9:26
KING
"SHALL HE APPEAR"
HEB.9:28
PROPHETIC
KINGLY
SANCTIFICATION
12 Teaching us that, denying ungodliness and worldly lusts, we should live soberly, righteously, and godly, in this present world;
JUSTIFICATION
11 For the grace of God that bringeth salvation hath appeared to all men,
GLORIFICATION
13 Looking for that blessed hope, and the glorious appearing of the great God and our Saviour Jesus Christ;
TITUS 2:11-12
"CREATIVE AGES"
THE THEOCRACY
THE KINGDOM
"AGES OF THE AGES"
THE CROSS
"SUFFERINGS"
I.PET.1:11
FIRST COMING
THE CHURCH
THE CROWN
ACTS 1:9-11
ZECH.14:4
"GLORY"
I.PET.1:11
SECOND COMING
THE NEW EARTH
THE FALL
BACKWARD TO "THE FALL"
THE ALTAR
FORWARD TO THE "CROSS"
BACKWARD TO THE "CROSS"
THE TABLE
"FOR AS OFTEN AS YE EAT THIS BREAD, AND DRINK THIS CUP, YE DO SHOW THE LORD'S DEATH---TILL HE COME"
I.COR.11:26
FORWARD TO THE "COMING"
BACKWARD TO THE "COMING"
THE THRONE
FORWARD TO THE DELIVERY OF THE KINGDOM
I.COR.15:24-28
THE TWO COMINGS
DESIGNED AND DRAWN BY
CLARENCE LARKIN, FOXCHASE, PHILA, PA,
COPYRIGHTED. 9/10/1918

The Second Coming of Christ

"In My Father's House are many mansions: if it were **not** so, I would have told you. **I go to prepare a place for you.** And if I go and prepare a place for you, **I WILL COME AGAIN, and receive you unto myself;** that where I am, there ye may be also." John 14:2-3.

There is no fact in history more clearly established than the fact of the "First Coming" of Christ. But as His "First Coming" did not fulfill all the prophecies associated with His "Coming," it is evident that there must be another "Coming" to completely fulfill them. It was because the religious leaders of Christ's day failed to distinguish between the prophecies that related to His "First Coming," and those that related to His "Second Coming" that they rejected Him. Peter tells us (I Pet. 1: 10, 11) that the prophets themselves did not clearly perceive the difference between the **"Sufferings"** and **"Glory"** of Christ. That is, they did not see that there was a **"TIME SPACE"** between the **"Cross"** and the **"Crown,"** and that the "Cross" would precede the "Crown." But we have no such excuse. We live on this side of the "Cross," and we can readily pick out all the prophecies that were fulfilled at Christ's "First Coming" and apply the remainder to His "Second Coming." It is clear then that Christ's "First Coming," important as it was, is not the "doctrinal centre" of the Scriptures, that is, Christ's "First Coming" was not the centre of a circle that contains all doctrine, but was one of the foci of an ellipse of which the other is the **"SECOND COMING."**

This is shown on Chart No. 1. The Chart takes in the whole Mediatorial Work of Christ, Prophetic, Priestly and Kingly. This is included in an ellipse, the foci of which are the "First" and "Second" Comings of Christ. The "Cross" represents His "First Coming" and the "Crown" His "Second Coming." Between the "Fall" and the "First Coming" we have the **"ALTAR,"** which points backward to the "Fall" and forward to the "Cross." Between the "Comings" we have the **"TABLE"** which points backward to the "Cross" and forward to the "Second Coming." Between the "Second Coming" and the surrender of the "Kingdom" we have the **"THRONE,"** which points backward to the "Second Coming" and forward to the surrendering of the "Kingdom." The Apostle Paul in his epistles clearly distinguishes between the "Comings" and their doctrinal significance. In his letter to the Hebrews he classifies Christ's "appearings" as "Hath He appeared" (Heb. 9: 26), "Now to appear" (Heb. 9: 24), "Shall He appear" (Heb. 9: 28). In his letter to Titus (Titus 2: 11, 12), he brings out the doctrinal significance of these "appearings." As a Prophet He died for our **"JUSTIFICATION,"** as a Priest He lives at the right hand of God not only as our Advocate, but our **"SANCTIFIER,"** and when He comes again as a King it will be for our **"GLORIFICATION."**

On Chart No. 2 we see how it was that the Old Testament Prophets failed to distinguish between the "First" and "Second" Comings. From the prophet's "view-point" he saw the Birth of Jesus, the

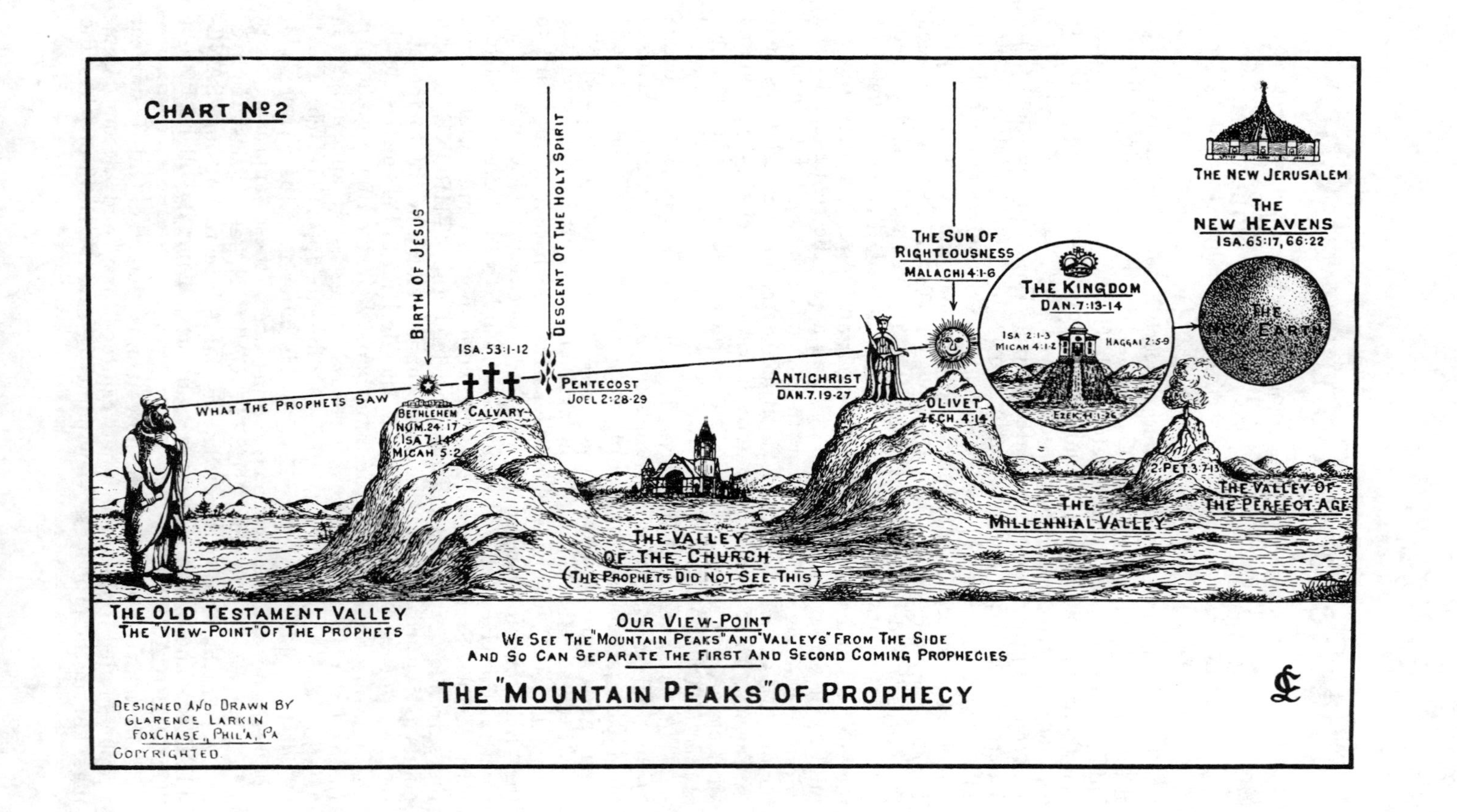

CHART Nº 2
BIRTH OF JESUS
DESCENT OF THE HOLY SPIRIT
ISA. 53:1-12
WHAT THE PROPHETS SAW
BETHLEHEM
NUM. 24:17
ISA 7:14
MICAH 5:2
CALVARY
PENTECOST
JOEL 2:28-29
ANTICHRIST
DAN. 7.19-27
OLIVET
ZECH. 4:14
THE SUN OF RIGHTEOUSNESS
MALACHI 4:1-6
THE KINGDOM
DAN. 7:13-14
ISA 2:1-3
MICAH 4:1-2
HAGGAI 2:5-9
THE NEW JERUSALEM
THE NEW HEAVENS
ISA. 65:17, 66:22
THE NEW EARTH
2 PET. 3:7-13
THE VALLEY OF THE PERFECT AGE
THE MILLENNIAL VALLEY
THE VALLEY OF THE CHURCH
(THE PROPHETS DID NOT SEE THIS)
THE OLD TESTAMENT VALLEY
THE "VIEW-POINT" OF THE PROPHETS
OUR VIEW-POINT
WE SEE THE "MOUNTAIN PEAKS" AND "VALLEYS" FROM THE SIDE
AND SO CAN SEPARATE THE FIRST AND SECOND COMING PROPHECIES
THE "MOUNTAIN PEAKS" OF PROPHECY
DESIGNED AND DRAWN BY
CLARENCE LARKIN
FOX CHASE, PHIL'A, PA
COPYRIGHTED

Crucifixion, the Outpouring of the Holy Spirit, the Antichrist, the Sun of Righteousness, the Millennial Kingdom, Ezekiel's Temple and the New Heavens and the New Earth, as "Mountain Peaks" of **one great mountain,** but we standing off to the side see these peaks as belonging to two different mountains with the "Valley of the Church" in between. And more we see that there are two more valleys, one, the "Millennial Valley," separates the "Second Coming" from the "Renovation of the Earth by Fire" (II Pet. 3:7-13), and the other is the Valley of the "Perfect Age."

While the First and Second Comings of Christ are separated by this Dispensation they are nevertheless not complete in themselves, the Second necessitated the First, and the First demands the Second. They are both necessary to complete the Plan of Salvation. The First Coming was for the salvation of my **"SOUL;"** the Second is for the salvation of my **"BODY,"** for there can be no resurrection of the body until Christ comes back.

THE SECOND COMING

I. AS TO THE FACT

1. THE TESTIMONY OF JESUS HIMSELF.

Matt 16:27. "For the Son of Man shall **come in the glory of his Father,** with his angels, and then he shall reward every man according to his work."

Matt. 25:31, 32. "When the Son of Man shall **come in his glory,** and all the holy angels with him, then shall he sit upon the 'Throne of His Glory;' and before him shall be gathered all nations; and he shall separate them one from another, as a shepherd divideth his sheep from the goats."

John 14:2, 3. "In my Father's house are many mansions; if it were not so I would have told you. I go to prepare a place for you. And if I go and prepare a place for you I will **come again,** and receive you unto myself; that where I am, there ye may be also."

John 21:22. "If I will that he tarry till **I come** what is that to thee? Follow thou me."

2. THE TESTIMONY OF HEAVENLY BEINGS.

Acts 1:10, 11. "And while they looked steadfastly toward heaven as he went up, behold, two **men** stood by them in white apparel; which also said, Ye men of Galilee, why stand ye gazing up into heaven? This **SAME JESUS,** which is taken up from you into heaven, shall so come **IN LIKE MANNER** as ye have seen him go into heaven."

This passage declares that the **SAME JESUS** shall return **IN LIKE MANNER** as He went, that is, that His return will be **visible** and **personal.** The two **"men"** that "stood by" were probably Moses and Elijah. They appeared with Jesus on the Mt. of Transfiguration, they were doubtless the **"two men"** who testified to the women at the tomb that Jesus had risen (Luke 24:4, 5), and they will be the **"Two Witnesses"** that shall testify during the Tribulation. Rev. 11:3-12.

3. THE TESTIMONY OF THE APOSTLES

PAUL—"For our conversation is in heaven; **from whence also we look for the Saviour,** the Lord Jesus Christ, who shall change our vile body, that it may be fashioned like unto his glorious body, according to the working whereby he is able even to subdue all things unto himself." Phil. 3:20, 21.

"Looking for that **'Blessed Hope'** and the **'Glorious Appearing'** of the great God and our Saviour Jesus Christ." Titus 2:13.

"So Christ was once offered to bear the sins of many; and unto them that look for him shall he appear the **'Second Time'** without sin unto salvation." Heb. 9:28.

JAMES—"Be patient therefore, brethren, unto the **coming of the Lord.**" James 5:7.

PETER—"For we have not followed cunningly devised fables when we made known unto you the power and **coming** of our Lord Jesus Christ, but were eye-witnesses of his majesty." II Pet. 1:16.

Peter here refers to the Transfiguration of Christ on the mount (Matt. 17:1-5), which was a type of His Second Coming. Moses was a type of the "resurrection saints," and Elijah of those who shall be translated without dying. Peter, James and John were a type of the Jewish Remnant that shall see Him when He comes, and the remaining disciples at the foot of the mount, unable to cast the demon out of the boy, of those professed followers of Jesus who shall be left behind at the Rapture, and who shall be powerless to cast the demons out of the demon-possessed people of that period.

JUDE—"And Enoch also, the seventh from Adam, prophesied of these, saying, Behold, the Lord cometh with ten thousand of his saints, to execute judgment upon all, and to convince all that are ungodly among them of all their ungodly deeds which they have ungodly committed, and of all their hard speeches which ungodly sinners have spoke against him." Jude 14:15.

JOHN—"And now, little children, abide in him; that, when he shall appear we may have confidence, and not be ashamed before him **at his coming.**" I John 2:28.

"Behold, he **cometh with clouds**; and every eye shall see him, and they also which pierced him, and all kindreds of the earth shall wail because of him." Even so, Amen. Rev. 1:7.

4. THE TESTIMONY OF THE LORD'S SUPPER.

"For as often as ye eat this bread, and drink this cup, ye do show the Lord's death **till he come.**" I Cor. 11:26.

The Lord's Supper is not a permanent ordinance. It will be discontinued when the Lord returns. It is a Memorial Feast. It looks back to the "Cross" and forward to the "Coming." An engagement ring is not intended to be permanent. It is simply a pledge of mutual love and loyalty, and gives place to the wedding ring. So the Lord's Table may be looked upon as a betrothal pledge left to the Church during the absence of her betrothed.

Paul in all his epistles refers but 13 times to Baptism, while he speaks of the Lord's return 50 times. One verse in every 30 in the New Testament refers to Christ's Second Coming. There are 20 times as many references in the Old Testament to Christ's Second Coming as to His First Coming.

THE FIVE THEORIES

While the majority of professing Christians admit **the fact of the** Second Coming of Christ, they are not agreed as to the **"manner"** or **"time."** There are five theories as to the Second Coming.

1. **That His Coming Again Is "SPIRITUAL" and Was Fulfilled at Pentecost.**

It was not Christ but the Holy Spirit that came at Pentecost, and his coming was conditioned on Christ's **absence,** for Jesus said, "It is expedient for you that I **go away**; for if I **go not away,** the Comforter (H. S.) will not come unto you; but if I **DEPART,** I will **SEND HIM UNTO YOU."** John 16:7. If the Holy Spirit is only another manifestation of Christ, then they are identical, and that **NULLIFIES THE TRINITY.** The fact is, the whole New Testament was written **after** Pentecost, and declares over 150 times that the Second Coming of Christ was still **future.** And more, none of the events predicted as accompanying the Second Coming occurred at Pentecost, such as the **Resurrection of the "Dead in Christ,"** the **Translation of the "Living Saints,"** the **"Binding of Satan,"** etc.

2. **That the "CONVERSION OF THE SINNER" is the Coming of the Lord.**

This cannot be, for at conversion the sinner comes to Christ, not Christ to the sinner; and the sinner's conversion is the work of the Holy Spirit, and not the work of Christ. It is true that there is such a thing as the spiritual **indwelling of Christ** in the believer, but His Second Coming, like His First Coming is to be an **outward, visible, personal coming.**

3. **That "DEATH" is the Coming of the Lord.**

The text that is used more than any other for funeral sermons is —"Watch, therefore; for ye know neither the day nor the hour wherein the Son of Man cometh." Matt. 25:13. The context shows that this refers to a future coming of Christ. Christ could not come to the earth every time a person dies for two reasons—

(1) A soul passes into eternity every second, and this would necessitate Christ's remaining continuously on the earth.

(2) Christ is engaged in His High Priestly functions in the Heavenlies, and could not leave them to come to the earth for the souls of the dying.

The fact is, that at death the believer goes to Christ. Christ does **not** come for him. Death is always spoken of as a departure. "Absent **from the** body, **present** (at home) with the Lord." II Cor. 5:6-8.

If Jesus had meant by His Second Coming **"Death,"** He would have said to His Disciples—"If I go and prepare a place for you, I will send 'Death' to bring you to myself," but He did not. He said—**"I will come again** and receive you unto myself." The last chapter of John's Gospel settles the matter. Peter said to Jesus—"Lord, and what shall this man (referring to John) do? Jesus saith unto him, If I will that he tarry **till I come,** what is that to thee? Follow thou me. Then went this saying abroad among the brethren, that that disciple (John) **should not DIE."** John 21:21-23. We see from this that the Disciples did not think that the "Coming of the Lord" meant "death." There was a great difference between these two things in their mind. Death is an enemy (I Cor. 15:26, 55), it holds us in the grave, it robs the body of its attractiveness, it is the "Wages of Sin" (Rom. 6:23), and the result of God's wrath, while the Second Coming of Christ is a manifestation of His love. Christ is the "Prince of Life." There can be no death where He is. Death flees at His coming. When He was on earth nothing could remain dead in His presence. His Coming is not death but resurrection. He is the **"Resurrection"** and the **"Life,"** and when He Comes, He will change our **vile body,** that it may be fashioned like unto His "Glorious Body." Phil. 3:20, 21.

4. **That the "DESTRUCTION OF JERUSALEM" in A. D. 70 by the Romans Was the Second Coming of the Lord.**

The Lord was not present at the destruction of Jerusalem. It was destroyed by Roman soldiers, and none of the things that are to occur at the "Second Coming" occurred at the destruction of Jerusalem, such as the resurrection of the dead, the translation of living saints, and the physical changes that are to occur at Jerusalem and in the land of Palestine at Christ's coming. Zech. 14:4-11. Ez. 47:1-12. Christ's purpose in coming back is not to **destroy** Jerusalem, but to **RESTORE** it. It must be trodden down of the Gentiles until the "Times of the Gentiles" are fulfilled, **"then** shall they see the Son of Man coming in a cloud with power and great glory." Luke 21:24-28. The Book of Revelation, **written 26 years after the destruction of Jerusalem,** speaks of the Second Coming of Christ as still **future.**

5. **That the "DIFFUSION OF CHRISTIANITY" is the Second Coming of the Lord.**

This cannot be true, for the "Diffusion of Christianity" is **gradual,** whereas the Scriptures declare that the "Return of the Lord" shall be **SUDDEN** and **UNEXPECTED,** as a "Thief in the Night." Matt. 24:27, 36, 42, 44. I Thess. 5:2. Rev. 3:3. Again the "Diffusion of Christianity" is a **process,** while the Scriptures invariably speak of the "Return of the Lord" as an **EVENT.** The diffusion of Christianity brings **Salvation** to the wicked, whereas the "Return of the Lord" is said to bring not salvation but **SUDDEN DESTRUCTION.** I. Thess. 5:2, 3; II Thess. 1:7-10.

II. AS TO THE TIME

Of the exact time we cannot be certain. When Jesus was on the earth He said—"But of that day and that hour knoweth no man, no, not the angels which are in heaven, neither (not yet) the Son, but the Father." Mark 13:32. After His Resurrection and before His Ascension, He refused to satisfy the curiosity of His Disciples, saying to them—"It is not for you to know the **'times'** or the **'seasons'** which the Father hath put in his own power." Acts 1:7. Jesus knew of Daniel's prophecy of the "Seventy Weeks" (Dan. 9:20-27), but He fixed no dates for their fulfillment. The student of prophecy is not to be a "date-setter," but he is to **watch.** "Signs" are for the Jew. There is nothing to prevent Christ coming for His Church at any time.

While we do not know the day or the hour of Christ's Coming **we know** that it will be

PRE-MILLENNIAL.

By Pre-Millennial we mean before the Millennium. That is, before the period of a **"Thousand Years"** spoken of in Rev. 20:1-6. This period is spoken of in other scriptures as "The Kingdom," and is described in glowing terms by the prophets as a time when the earth shall be blessed with a universal rule of righteousness. The passage in Rev. 20:1-6 simply tells us that the length of the period shall be 1000 years.

The very structure of the New Testament demands that Christ shall return **before** the Millennium. Here are a few reasons.

1. When Christ comes He will **RAISE THE DEAD,** but the Righteous dead are to be raised **BEFORE** the Millennium, that they may reign with Christ during the 1000 years, hence there can be no Millennium before Christ comes. Rev. 20:5.

2. When Christ comes He will **SEPARATE THE "TARES" FROM THE "WHEAT,"** but as the Millennium is a period of **UNIVERSAL RIGHTEOUSNESS** the separation of the "Tares" and "Wheat" must take place **BEFORE** the Millennium, therefore there can be no Millennium before Christ comes. Matt. 13:40-43.

3. When Christ comes Satan **SHALL BE BOUND,** but as Satan is to be bound **during** the Millennium, there can be no Millennium until Christ comes. Rev. 20:1-3.

4. When Christ comes Antichrist is to be **DESTROYED,** but as Antichrist is to be destroyed **before** the Millennium there can be no Millennium until Christ comes. II Thess. 2:8; Rev. 19:20.

5. When Christ comes the Jews are to be **RESTORED TO THEIR OWN LAND,** but as they are to be restored to their own land **BEFORE** the Millennium, there can be no Millennium before Christ comes. Ez. 36:24-28; Rev. 1:7 (Zech. 12:10).

6. When Christ comes it will be **unexpectedly,** and we are commanded to watch lest He take us **unawares.** Now if He is not coming until AFTER the Millennium, and the Millennium is **not yet here,** why command us to watch for an event that is over **1000 years off?**

III. AS TO THE MANNER

He will return in the **SAME MANNER** as He went. Acts 1:11. He went up **BODILY** and **VISIBLY** and He shall come in like manner. He went in a cloud, and He will return in a cloud. "Behold, He cometh with the **clouds**; and **every eye shall see Him,** and they also which pierced Him; and all kindreds of the earth shall wail because of Him." Rev. 1:7. The only difference will be that He went up alone, He will return as a King (Luke 19:12), followed by a retinue of the angelic hosts. "For the Son of Man shall come in the glory of His Father **with his angels**; and then He shall reward every man according **to his works."** Matt. 16:27. His "Return" however will be in

TWO STAGES

He will come first into the region of our atmosphere, and the **"dead in Christ,"** and the **"living saints"** shall be **"caught up"** to meet Him **"IN THE AIR."** Then after the risen and translated saints have been judged and rewarded for their works, and they, as the Church, the Bride of Christ, have been married to Him, He will come **with them** to the earth and land on the Mount of Olives, the place from whence He ascended. "And His feet shall stand in that day upon the Mount of Olives, which is before Jerusalem on the east, and the Mount of Olives shall cleave in the midst thereof toward the east and toward the west, and there shall be a very great valley; and half of the mountain shall remove toward the north, and half of it toward the south." Zech. 14:4.

The First Stage of His Return is called **"THE RAPTURE;"** the Second Stage—**"THE REVELATION."** The time between the two Stages is not less than seven years, and is occupied in the heavens **by the "JUDGMENT OF BELIEVERS FOR WORKS,"** and on the earth by **"THE GREAT TRIBULATION."** See Chart No. 4, p. 36.

THE RAPTURE

The Rapture is described in I. Thess. 4:15-17. "For this we say **unto** you by the word of the Lord, that we which are alive and remain unto the coming of the Lord shall not prevent them which are asleep. For the Lord **HIMSELF** shall descend from heaven with a **shout,** with the **voice of the Archangel** (Michael) and with the **trump of God**; and the **DEAD IN CHRIST shall rise first**; then we which are **ALIVE AND REMAIN** (saints only) shall be caught up together **with** them in the clouds, to meet the Lord **IN THE AIR,** and so shall we ever be with the Lord."

From this we see that "The Rapture" will be **twofold.**

1. The Resurrection of the **"DEAD IN CHRIST."**
2. The Translation of the **"LIVING SAINTS."**

This twofold character of "The Rapture" Jesus revealed to Martha **when** He was about to raise her brother Lazarus. He said to her.

"I am the 'Resurrection and the Life,' he that believeth in **Me, though he were dead** yet shall he **LIVE** (First Resurrection Saints); and whosoever **LIVETH** (is alive when I come back) and believeth in Me shall **NEVER DIE."** John 11:25, 26. This twofold character of The Rapture, Paul emphasizes in his immortal chapter on the Resurrection.

"Behold, I show you a **Mystery,** we shall not all **Sleep,** but **we** shall **All Be Changed** in a moment, in the twinkling of an eye, at the last trump; for the trumpet shall sound, and the **dead** shall be **raised,** and **we** shall be **changed.** For this **Corruptible** (the dead in Christ) must put on **incorruption,** and this **mortal** (the living saints) must put on **immortality.** So when this **corruptible** shall have put on **incorruption,** and this **mortal** shall have put on **immortality,** then shall be brought to pass the saying that is written, **DEATH IS SWALLOWED UP IN VICTORY.**

O DEATH, WHERE IS THY STING?
O GRAVE, WHERE IS THY VICTORY?"
I. Cor. 15: 51-57.

The last two lines refer only to those who are "changed without dying," for it is only those who will not die who can shout—

"O Death, Where Is Thy Sting?
"O Grave, Where Is Thy Victory?"

In II Cor. 5: 1-4, Paul expresses his longing, and the longing of the Saints, to be among those who should not be "unclothed" by Death, but who should be "clothed upon" by Immortality "without dying."

"For we know that if our earthly house of this tabernacle (the body), were **dissolved** (that is die), we have a building of God, an house not made with hands eternal in the heavens. For in this (body) we groan, earnestly desiring to be 'clothed upon' with our house which is from heaven; if so be that being 'clothed' we shall not be found naked. For we that are in this tabernacle (the body) do groan, being burdened; not for that we would be **'unclothed'** (by death), but **'clothed upon'** (by immortality), that 'mortality' might be swallowed up of life."

In his letter to the Philippians, while Paul hopes that—

"If by any means he may attain unto The (out from among the dead) **Resurrection,** yet he pressed toward the mark for the **'prize'** of the **High** (out and up) **Calling of God** in Christ Jesus." Phil. 3: 11-14.

That is, while Paul would esteem it a great thing to "rise from the dead" at the First Resurrection, and be "caught up" with those who should be "changed," yet he would esteem it a "prize" if he could be caught up "without dying," that is, live until Jesus came back.

THE RAPTURE WILL BE A "SURPRISE"

"Watch therefore; for ye know not what hour your Lord doth come. But know this, that if the goodman of the house had known in what watch the thief would come, he would have watched, and would not have suffered his house to be broken up. Therefore be ye also ready; for **in such an hour as ye think not the Son of Man COMETH."** Matt. 24: 42-44. "Behold, I come as a thief. Blessed is he that watcheth, and keepeth his garments, lest he walk naked, and they see his shame." Rev. 16: 15. "But of the **'times'** and the **'seasons'** brethren, ye have no need that I write unto you. For yourselves know perfectly that the 'Day of the Lord' (the day of His Return), so cometh **as a thief in the night.** For when they shall say, **'Peace and Safety;'** then sudden destruction cometh upon them as travail upon a woman with child, and they shall not escape." This refers to the Second Stage of Christ's Coming, the "Revelation," when He shall take vengeance upon His enemies. II Thess. 1:7-10. But Paul adds—"But ye, brethren, are not in darkness, that **that day** (the day of His Return) should overtake **you** as a thief." I Thess. 5:1-4.

We see from this that when Christ comes back it will be when we are not expecting Him. He will come as a thief comes. A thief does not announce his coming. He comes for a certain purpose. He does not take everything there is in the house. He takes only the precious things, the jewels, the gold, the silver and fine wearing apparel. He does not come to stay. As soon as he secures what he is after he departs. So Jesus at the Rapture will come and take away the saints only. The thief leaves much more than he takes. He leaves the house and the furniture and the household utensils. So the Lord at the Rapture will leave the wicked and the great mass of the heathen behind for those who will be taken will be comparatively few.

We must not forget in our study of this subject that there are to be **two** resurrections of the dead. The first, of the Righteous dead **before** the Millennium, and the second of the Wicked dead **after** the Millennium. Rev. 20:4-6. The subject cannot be treated fully in this pamphlet but will be found in the author's larger work on "Dispensational Truth," in the chapters on "The Resurrection" and "Spirit World" with charts.

THE RAPTURE WILL BE "ELECTIVE"

It will not only separate the saints from unbelievers, but it will separate husbands from wives, brothers from sisters, friends from friends.

"I tell you, in that night there shall be two men in one bed; the one shall be taken, and the other shall be left. Two women shall be grinding together; the one shall be taken, and the other left. Two men shall be in the field; the one shall be taken, and the other left." Luke 17:34-36. The words "men" and "women" in this passage are in italics. That means that they are not in the original, and so the passage should read there shall be "two in one bed," husband and wife, or two brothers, or two sisters, or two friends. Two in "bed" indicates night; two grinding at the mill, morning or evening; two in the field mid-noon. This shows that the Rapture will happen all over the earth at the same time or as the Apostle describes it in a **"moment,"** or the **"twinkling of an eye."** "As the lightning cometh out of the east, and shineth even unto the west; so shall also the **coming of the Son of Man Be"** (Matt. 24:27) is the way Jesus puts it.

The "Rapture" will be the most startling "event" of this Age and Dispensation. As it is to occur in the **"twinkling of an eye"** and **all over the earth at the same time,** that part of the world that is not asleep will witness the event. As to the **"Shout of the Lord," the**

"Voice of the Archangel," and the **"Trump of God"** we do not know whether their sound will be heard and distinguished by others than the "dead in Christ" and the "living saints." We know that one day the Father spoke to Christ in a voice that He understood, but the people who stood by mistook it for "thunder." John 12:28, 29. When the Lord appeared to Saul of Tarsus on the road to Damascus and spoke to him, the men that journeyed with him stood speechless, "hearing a voice," but seeing no man, and not understanding what was said. Acts 9:3-7. We know however that the "dead in Christ" will hear the sound, for it will be "intensely penetrating." There will be no graves so deep, no catacombs so rock covered, no pyramids or mausoleums so thick, but what the sound shall reach their depths and the "dead in Christ" shall hear the cry—**"awake ye sleeping saints and arise from the dead, it is MORNING, the morning of the FIRST RESURRECTION."**

On the morning of that glorious day the air will be filled with the "spirits" of the "Dead in Christ," come back to earth to get their bodies, raised and glorified. Whether the cemeteries and country church yards will look like ploughed fields, and monuments and grave slabs be overturned and vaults and places of sepulchre be shattered by the exodus of those who found their last resting place there, and thus testify to the fact of the **literal bodily resurrection of the dead,** or whether the sainted dead shall slip out of their sepulchres without disturbing them, as Christ arose and left the tomb without breaking the seal, the angel rolling away the stone simply to show that the tomb was empty, we are not told, only the event itself will disclose the manner of the First Resurrection.

If the dead slip out of their places of sepulchre without disturbing them, the First Resurrection will be secret and probably unknown to the world, but it will not be so with the "Living Saints" who are translated. If it is night on our side of the globe when the Rapture occurs the community will wake up in the morning to find all the real Christians gone, disappeared in the night. Many may hear the **sound** of the "Midnight cry"—

"BEHOLD THE BRIDEGROOM COMETH,"

but thinking it only thunder, will turn over for another nap, but in the morning they will find the bedroom door locked, with the key on the inside, just as they locked it before retiring, and the clothes of the loved one who occupied the room with them lying where they were placed when taken off the night before, but that loved one, who was a Christian, missing. Husbands will wake up to find that Christian wives are gone, and wives will wake up to find Christian husbands gone. Brothers and sisters will be missed, and dear children absent, and not an infant will be left behind. Many faithful servants and employes will not report for duty, and the world will awake to the fact that the Bible is true, and the much despised doctrine of the Pre-Millennial Coming of the Lord to gather out His saints is no fanciful interpretation of Scripture.

If it be **day** with us when the Rapture occurs, the **"EVENT"** will be **startling.** As it was in the days of Noah (Matt. 24:36-39), the people will be eating and drinking, marrying and giving in marriage, buying and selling, planting and building.

If it be at a pleasant time of the year, the boats, and cars, and parks will be filled with pleasure seekers. If it be in the midst of the week, and during the business hours of the day, the shops and stores will be filled with shoppers and the mills with toilers, and the streets of the cities lined with men and women and children on pleasure and business bent. Suddenly a noise from heaven will be heard like a great peal of thunder. The people will rush to doors and windows, and those on the streets and in the fields will look up to see what has happened. To the vast majority it will be but a startling and alarming **sound,** but to many it will be the

"VOICE OF THE LORD."

But when the people recover from their surprised and affrighted condition they will discover that a great many people are missing, and that the missing were the best people in the community. The large Department Stores, Banking Institutions, Manufacturing Plants, and other places of business will find their working force depleted by the loss of faithful employes. People walking on the streets will find their companions gone, and the street car lines will be blocked because of absent motormen, conductors and teamsters. Railroad and steamboat lines will be crippled, and confusion will reign everywhere. In many homes the servants will be missing and members of the family will come home to find loved ones gone.

At first the whole thing will be a **Mystery,** until some one who had heard or read about the "Rapture of the Saints," realizing what has happened, will explain the situation.

But one of the surprises of that day will be that so many professing Christians, and among them many ministers and Christian workers, will be left behind, while some who were not known to be Christians will be missing. The next day's papers will be full of what happened the day before, and many of them will be swelled to twice their ordinary size by the pressure on their advertising columns for information as to missing ones, and for help to fill important vacancies and positions of trust. For a few days the excitement will be intense. Then the people will settle down to the inevitable. With the exception of a few who will repent and turn to God, the mass of the people will become more hardened and wicked than before, and some who lost loved ones will be embittered. As the Holy Spirit will have gone back with the "Raptured Ones," and the "Saints," the **SALT** of the earth, been taken out, there will be nothing to prevent the rapid degeneration and **"Moral Putrefaction"** of those who are **"left,"** and sin and iniquity and all manner of crime and worldliness will increase and pave the way for the manifestation of Antichrist, under whose administration the world will rapidly ripen for judgment.

WHO ARE TO BE TAKEN

Some claim that **"all"** the Church are to pass **through the Tribulation** (see Chart 4) ; others that **"all"** the Church are to be caught out **before** the Tribulation, while some claim that only the "waiting" and

THE WISE VIRGINS
"They That Were Ready Went in with Him to the Marriage and the Door Was Shut."
Matt. 25: 10.

"Watching" Saints shall be caught out before the Tribulation, and that the rest must pass through it. The latter base their claim on Heb. 9: 28, where it says—"Unto them that **look for Him** shall He appear the second time without sin unto salvation." While this might apply to the living when He appears, it certainly cannot apply to the **dead.** There are tens and hundreds of thousands who "fell asleep in Jesus" who never heard of the Premillennial Coming of the Lord, or at least never grasped its meaning, and who therefore never "watched" and "waited" and "looked" for His Appearing. They surely are "In Christ"; and the "Dead in Christ" are to rise at the Rapture. Paul does not say in I Thess. 4: 16, 17, that it will be the "dead" who "watched" and "waited" and "looked," and those who are "alive" and "watch" and "wait" and "look" for His Appearing that shall be "caught out," but the dead **"In Christ,"** and we who **"Are Alive And Remain."**

The order of the Resurrection is—"Christ the 'First Fruits,' afterward they that 'are Christ's at His Coming.' " Paul says—"Behold, I show you a Mystery; we shall not all 'sleep,' but we shall **ALL Be Changed."** I Cor. 15: 51.

Then there is another fact that we must not forget, and that is, the **Unity** of the Church.

"For as the **Body Is One,** and hath many members, and **ALL the Members Of That One Body, Being Many ARE ONE BODY**; so also is Christ. For by **One Spirit** are we **ALL Baptized Into One Body."** I Cor. 12: 12, 13.

All then who have been "born again" (John 3: 3-7) are part of Christ's "Body," and we cannot conceive of Christ's "Body" being divided; part of it remaining "asleep" in the grave, and part of it "raised in glory"; part of it left to pass through the Tribulation, and part of it "changed" and caught up to meet Him in the air.

If "all" the Church are to pass through the Tribulation, then instead of waiting and watching "for the Lord," we should be waiting and watching "for the Tribulation," which is contrary to the teaching of Christ Himself. Matt. 24: 42-44.

The Tribulation is not for the perfecting "of the Saints." It has nothing to do with the Church. It is the time of "Jacob's Trouble" (Jer. 30: 7), and is the "Judgment of Israel," and it is God's purpose to keep the Church **Out Of It.** Rev. 2: 10. The Book of Revelation is written in chronological order. After the fourth chapter the Church is seen no more upon the earth until she appears in the nineteenth chapter coming with the Bridegroom "from" Heaven. The entire time between these two chapters is filled with appalling judgments that fall upon those that "dwell on the earth," and as the Church is not of the earth, but is supposed to "sit together in 'Heavenly Places' in Christ Jesus" (Eph. 2: 6), she will not be among those who "dwell on the earth" in those days.

The confusion is largely due to the fact that students of Prophetic Truth do not distinguish between Christ's coming **FOR** His Saints, and **WITH** His Saints. The former is called the "Rapture," the latter the "Revelation."

Numerous passages in scripture speak of Christ coming "with" His Saints (Zech. 14: 5, Col. 3: 4, I Thess. 3: 13, I Thess. 4: 14, Jude 14), but it is evident that they cannot come "with" Him, if they had not been previously caught out "to" Him. All such passages refer therefore to the "Revelation" and not the "Rapture."

The typical teaching of the Scriptures demand that the Church be caught out "before" the Tribulation. Joseph was a type of Christ and he was espoused to, and married Asenath, a Gentile bride, during the time of his "rejection by his brethren," and "before the famine," which typified the Tribulation, because it was the time of "Judgment of his Brethren." This is the time of Christ's rejection by "His Brethren"—the Jews, and to complete the type He must get His Bride—the church, "before" the Tribulation.

Moses, who is also a type of Christ, got his bride, and she a Gentile, "after" his rejection by his brethren, and "before" they passed through the Tribulation under Pharoah. Ex. 2: 23-25.

Enoch, a type of the "Translation Saints," was caught out "before" the Flood, and the Flood is a type of the Tribulation, and Noah and his family of the "Jewish Remnant" or 144,000 sealed ones of Rev. 7: 1-8, who will be preserved through the Tribulation.

How thrilling the thought that some of us shall not die, that in a moment, in the "twinkling of an eye" without being unclothed by the ghastly hands of Death, and instead of the winding sheet of the grave, we shall be instantly changed and clothed with the glorious garments of immortality. What a transport of joy will fill our being as we suddenly feel the thrill of immortality throbbing through our veins, and find ourselves being transported through the air in the company of fellow Christians and of our loved ones who fell asleep in Jesus. What welcome recognitions and greetings there will be as we journey up with them to the "Bridal Halls of Heaven," where we shall join in the new and triumphal song of Moses and the Lamb. Rev. 5: 9, 10.

WHAT WILL BECOME OF THOSE WHO ARE LEFT BEHIND?

This is a sad question, but it is eagerly asked by many. What saith the Lord?

> "Then said one unto Him, Lord, are there **FEW that be saved?** And He said unto them, Strive to enter in at the strait (narrow) gate: for many, I say unto you, will seek to enter in (when He comes), and shall not be able, when once the **'Master of the House'** is risen up, and hath **SHUT THE DOOR,** and ye begin to stand without, and to knock at the door, saying, Lord, open unto us; and He shall answer and say unto you, **I know not whence ye are:** then shall ye begin to say, We have eaten and drunk in Thy presence, and Thou hast taught in our streets. But He shall say, I tell you, **I KNOW YOU NOT WHENCE YE ARE; DEPART FROM ME, ALL YE WORKERS OF INIQUITY."** Luke 13: 23-27.

The time of the closing of the door is revealed in the Parable of the "Ten Virgins." It will be when the Bridegroom comes, and those

THE FOOLISH VIRGINS
"Too Late! Too Late! Ye Cannot Enter Now."

that **are ready** (the "Wise Virgins") have gone in with Him to the "Marriage." When the "Foolish Virgins" come later, and say—"Lord, open to us," He will answer—**"I KNOW YOU NOT."** That is, I **never knew you.** You were only mere professors. Then follow the words—"Watch therefore (be ready), for ye know neither the day nor the hour wherein the Son of Man cometh." Matt. 25:1-13. Note that the persons shut out are not those who never heard the Gospel, but those who had been professing followers of Jesus, who had eaten and drunk in His presence and even gone out to meet Him.

It may readily be supposed that the taking away of loved ones at the Rapture will cause many of those left behind to seek the Lord, but as the Holy Spirit goes back with the Church, and for the time being ceases His Office Work of Regeneration, who is to convert those who are left? There is a passage in Hebrews that has troubled many a sincere soul who has feared that they had committed the "Unpardonable Sin." It is this—

> "For if we sin (continue to sin) **wilfully** after that we have received the knowledge (that is know about it) of the truth, there remaineth no more sacrifice for sins, but a certain fearful looking for of judgment and fiery indignation, which shall devour the adversaries." Heb. 10:26.

The preceding verse shows that this warning is connected with the Lord's Coming—"So much the more, as ye see **'The Day' approaching**—the **"DAY OF THE LORD."** The expression—**"there remaineth no more sacrifice for sins,"** implies that those who thus sin against their knowledge are without hope.

That there will be a "Great Multitude" saved after the Church is "caught out" in the "Time Space" between the "Rapture" and the "Revelation," is clearly revealed in Rev. 7:9-17, and some of them may be of those **"left behind,"** but they will have to pass through great tribulation and suffer a martyr's death for refusing to worship the "Image of the Beast." Rev. 13:11-17. And we read that—When the Lord Jesus shall be revealed (at the close of the Great Tribulation) from Heaven with His mighty angels, in **"flaming fire"** He shall take vengeance on them that **"KNOW NOT GOD,"** and that **"OBEY NOT THE GOSPEL OF OUR LORD JESUS CHRIST."** II Thess. 1:7-10. Let us not run the risk of being left behind.

WHAT HAPPENS BETWEEN THE RAPTURE AND REVELATION

After the Saints are "caught out" they are to be judged. This judgment takes place at the "Judgment Seat of Christ." The Scriptures speak of five separate Judgments. They differ in five general aspects. As to **"Subjects," "Time," "Place," "Basis of Judgment"** and **"Result."** For a complete description of these Judgments see **my** larger Book on **"Dispensational Truth."**

The judgment of the Believer is **threefold.** At the Cross as **a** "Sinner" for **sin**; this is **Past**. John 5: 24. As a "Son;" this is **Present,** and consists of "self-judgment" and confession, or else the punishment of chastisement. I Cor. 11: 31, 32. As a "Servant;" this is **future,** and is a Judgment for "Works" at the

"JUDGMENT SEAT OF CHRIST"

"We **must** all appear before the 'Judgment Seat of Christ,' that every one may receive the things 'done in the body' according to that **he hath done,** whether it be 'good' or 'bad' (worthless)." II Cor. 5: 10.

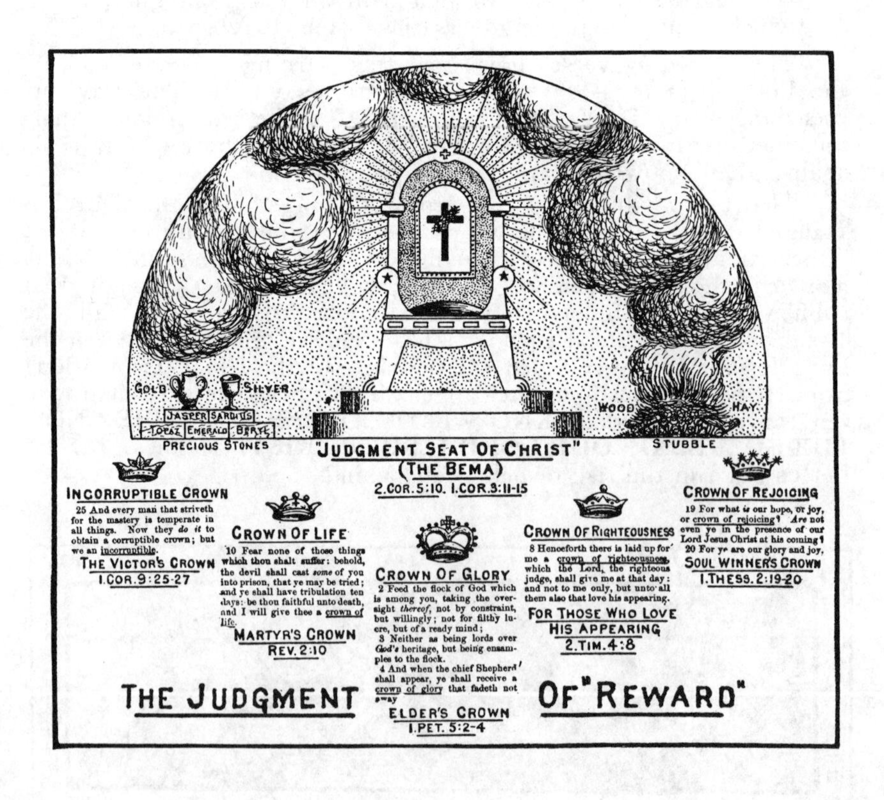

The pronoun "We" occurs 26 times in the chapter, and in every instance it means the Believer, and the Epistle is addressed to the "Church" and "Saints" at Corinth, so the Judgment here spoken of is for Believers "only." The "Time" of this Judgment is when the Lord comes (I Cor. 4:5), and the "Place" is "in the air" (I Thess. 4:17) and before the Judgment Seat of Christ.

It will not be a Judgment in the sense of a "trial" to see whether the judged are innocent (saved) or guilty (lost), for it is a Judgment of the "saved only." It will be like the Judges' stand at a Fair, or Race Track, where rewards are distributed to the successful contestants. Paul describes such a scene in I Cor. 9:24-27.

It is not a Judgment for sin, but for "works." This Judgment is described in I Cor. 3:11-15.

"Other foundation can no man lay than that is laid, which is Jesus Christ. Now if any man build upon this foundation **gold, silver, precious stones** (valuable building stones, as marble, etc.), **wood, hay stubble**; every man's 'Work' shall be made manifest; for the 'Day' (Judgment Day) shall declare it, because it shall be revealed by 'fire,' and the fire shall try every man's 'work' of what sort it is. If any man's work 'abide' which he hath built there upon he shall receive a 'reward.' If any man's work shall be 'burned' he shall suffer 'loss;' but 'he himself shall be saved;' yet so as by fire."

The result of this Judgment is "reward" or "loss." All our "bad" and "dead works," represented by the wood, hay and stubble, will be consumed, and only our "good works" shall remain. There is much which passes for Christian service which is merely human and secular, and does not count in our eternal reward. For those who deserve a "reward" it will be

The Crowning Day.

After the Grecian games were all over the runners, wrestlers, and successful contestants assembled before the "Bema," or Judges' stand, which was an elevated seat on which the Umpire sat, and the winners received a "corruptible crown" of "laurel leaves." Some had no reward, they had lost the "Victor's Crown." But while there was no reward there was no punishment, they were not cast out.

The New Testament speaks of Five Crowns.

1. **The Crown of "LIFE."**

This is the "Martyr's" crown, and is mentioned twice.

"Blessed is the man that endureth temptation (testing), for when he is 'tried' (at the Judgment Seat of Christ), he shall receive the **'Crown of Life'** which the Lord hath promised to them that love Him." James 1:12.

"Fear none of those things which thou shalt suffer; behold, the Devil shall cast some of you into prison, that ye may be tried (tested) and ye shall have tribulation ten days; be thou faithful 'unto death,' and I will give thee a **'Crown of Life.'"** Rev. 2:10.

Notice it does not say "until" death, but "unto" death. They were not to recant, but to remain faithful unto a martyr's death. To recant was to lose the crown. This refers to the martyrs of the Tribulation Period.

2. The Crown of "GLORY."

This is the "Elder's" or "Pastor's" crown, given by the Chief Shepherd when He shall appear. But it is not for those who serve for "filthy lucre" or "lord it over God's heritage." I Pet. 5:2-4.

3. The Crown of "REJOICING."

This is the "Soul Winner's" crown. Those brought to Jesus by us will be our "crown of rejoicing" at His Coming. I Thess. 2:19, 20. Phil. 4:1.

4. The Crown of "RIGHTEOUSNESS."

This is the crown of those who "love His appearing and will be given in 'that day' "—the Day of His Appearing. II Tim. 4:8.

5. The "INCORRUPTIBLE" Crown.

This is the "Victor's" crown, and is for those who "keep under their body." I Cor. 9:25-27. Who do not yield to their fleshly lusts. Who do not permit themselves to be diverted from the work for the Master by worldly amusements and pleasure, nor saturate their body with drugs.

If we do not want to be **"ashamed at His Coming,"** I John 2:28, let us see to it that we keep our body "under" and so live that we shall secure a crown.

THE ROYAL WEDDING

After the Saints have been "caught out" and "judged," they, as the "Church," will become the "Bride of Christ."

The "Marriage" of the Church is prophetically referred to by Jesus in the Parable of the "Marriage of the King's Son" (Matt. 22: 1-14), and is consummated in Rev. 19:7-9.

"Let us be glad and rejoice and give honor to Him: for the

'Marriage of the Lamb'

is come, and His wife hath made herself ready. And to her was granted that she should be arrayed in fine linen, clean and white; for the fine linen is the righteousness of Saints. And he saith unto me, write, **Blessed are they which are called unto the MARRIAGE SUPPER OF THE LAMB."**

Notice that it does not say the "Marriage of the Bride," but the "Marriage of the **LAMB."** That grand event will be not so much the consummation of the hopes of the Bride, as it will be the consummation of the **plan of God for His Son,** arranged for **before the foundation of the World.** Eph. 1:4. The "Marriage of the Lamb" is the consummation of the joy of Christ as a **MAN.** It would not have been possible if Christ had not been born **in the flesh.** Otherwise it would have been the union of "dissimilar natures," for the "Bride" is of "human origin." This is why Jesus took His "human nature" back with Him to Heaven, and today we have in Heaven the **MAN** Christ Jesus. I Tim. 2:5.

While the "Bride" was chosen for Christ "before the foundation of the world," the "espousal" could not take place until Christ assumed humanity and ascended to Heaven as the **Man** Christ Jesus. There have been many long betrothals but Christ's has been the longest on record. **He has been waiting for His Bride nearly 1900 years, but He will not have to wait much longer. Soon Heaven shall resound with the cry—**

"**Let us be glad and rejoice, and give honor to Him, for the Marriage of the Lamb is Come.**" Rev. 19:7.

There have been many royal weddings of international interest, where the invited guests and spectators witnessed a spectacle magnificent in its appointments, and rejoiced in a union that bound together different nations. But the wedding of the Lamb and His Bride the Church will surpass them all, for it shall unite Heaven and Earth in a bond that shall never be broken, for what God (the Father) shall join together, no man shall ever put asunder, and that union no divorce shall ever break.

The Bride shall be "arrayed in fine linen, clean and white; for the fine linen is the righteousness of Saints." Rev. 19:7, 8. The word "righteousness" is plural, and should read "righteousnesses." Not the imputed righteousness of Christ, but the "righteous acts and works" of the saints themselves, that shall remain after they have passed through the "fiery test" of the "Judgment for Works" at the "Judgment Seat of Christ." I Cor. 3:11-15. What a contrast there will be between the purple and scarlet colored dress, and jewel bedecked person, of the "Harlot Wife" of Antichrist (Rev. 17:3, 4), and the spotless white robe of fine linen of the Bride of the Lamb.

During the time occupied by the "Judgment of Believers" and the Marriage of the Lamb in the Heavenlies, there will be awful times on the earth. The Jews will have, in large numbers, been gathered back to their own land, Palestine. About this time ten of the Nations occupying the territory of the old Roman Empire will enter into a Federation of Nations. Among the "Ten Kings" of those nations will arise the "Antichrist." He will soon prove himself to be a **"Great Ruler"** and will be made **PRESIDENT**. The Government will be a **"Democratic Monarchy."** The President will make a **"Covenant"** with the Jewish people. It may be a Covenant restoring to them their own land and recognizing their national existence. Whatever its character, the Prophet Isaiah speaks of it as a **"Covenant with DEATH and HELL."** Isa. 28:15. For 3½ years the President of the Federation will keep the Covenant. Then he will break it. For the balance of his reign 3½ years he will cause an awful persecution of the Jews, called by Jesus **"The Great Tribulation."** Matt. 24:21, 22. For a description of this period see my larger work.

In the Middle of this period, or at the time when Antichrist shall break the Covenant, there will be

WAR IN HEAVEN,

and Satan will be cast out into the earth and he will incarnate himself in Antichrist. Rev. 12:7-9. The Antichrist will then become known as **"THE BEAST,"** and a second Beast will arise (Rev. **13: 11-17**) called the **"FALSE PROPHET."** Rev. 16:13; 19:20. These three will make up the **"Satanic Trinity."** The Dragon (Satan) will be the **"Anti-God."** The Beast will be the **"Anti-Christ,"** and the False Prophet will be the "Anti-Spirit." See Chart Number 4.

The "Tribulation Period" of 3½ years will be the "Judgment of the Jews." As all of God's promises to the Jews are earthly, their Judgment must be earthly. This Judgment is a "National Judgment." For all their national sins God is going to make them **"Pass Under the Rod."** Ez. 20:34-38. He is going to cast them into his **"MELTING POT."** Ez. 22:19-22. Malachi 3:1-3. In the midst of their "fiery trials" in this time of **"Jacob's Trouble"** (Jer. 30:4-7; Dan. 12:1), they will cry to the Lord as they did amid the brick-kilns of Egypt and God will send them Him of whom Moses was a type, even the Lord Jesus, who shall then come **"with"** His Saints in the **"Second Stage"** of His Coming, the **Revelation,** and as He shall descend upon the Mount of Olives (Zech. 14:4), they shall look upon Him whom they "pierced" and a nation, the Jewish Nation, will be re-born in a day. Ezek. 36:24-27. Isa. 66:8.

When Christ comes **for** the Saints at the Rapture, He will be the **"Morning Star."** Rev. 22:16. When He comes **with** His Saints at the Revelation He will be the **"Sun of Righteousness."** Malachi 4:2. When Christ shall come back at the Revelation He shall find the armies of Antichrist gathered together at Armageddon (Rev. 16:13-16), and He shall destroy them with the **"Sword of His Mouth"** (Rev. 19:15, 20, 21), and the **"Beast"** and the **"False Prophet"** shall be cast **alive** into the **"Lake of Fire."** Then all the Gentile Nations will be summoned to the Valley of Jehoshaphat for judgment, and the "Son of Man" shall sit upon the

"THRONE OF HIS GLORY,"

a throne erected on the earth, and He shall judge the Nations for their treatment of His **brethren**—the **JEWS,** during the "Great Tribulation," and those nations that fed and clothed them and visited them when in prison will be known as the **"Sheep Nations,"** and He will say to them—"Come, ye blessed of my Father, inherit the Kingdom prepared for you from the foundation of the world." That Kingdom is the "Millennial Kingdom." But to the **"Goat Nations,"** the nations that neglected the Jews during the Tribulation, He will say—"Depart from Me, ye cursed, into everlasting fire, prepared for the Devil and his angels," and "these shall go away into everlasting punishment." Matt. 25:41-46. That is, the "Goat Nations" as **nations** will be destroyed, not one of them shall exist **as a nation** during the Millennium, and the wicked individuals that compose them will perish and be eternally lost. For a more full treatment see my **book** on "Dispensational Truth."

THE REVELATION

At the "Second Stage" of Christ's Second Coming, the "Revelation," we shall behold His **"Glory."** When Jesus came the first time He was disguised in the flesh. The "Incarnation" was the hiding of His Power, the veiling of His Deity. Now and then gleams of glory shot forth as on the Mt. of Transfiguration; but when He comes the Second Time we shall behold Him clothed with the glory He had with the Father before the world was. The "Revelation" will be as sudden and as unexpected as was the "Rapture." The sun will rise on that day strong and clear. Gentle breezes will waft themselves over the earth. There will be no signs of a storm or of the coming Judgment. The people will be buying and selling, building and planting, eating and drinking, marrying and giving in marriage. The statesmen will be revolving in their minds new plans for the world's betterment. The philanthropic will be devising new ways to help the people. The pleasure-loving will be seeking new sources of pleasure. The wicked will be plotting dark deeds; and the unbelieving will be proving to their own satisfaction that there is no God, no heaven, no hell, no coming judgment, when suddenly there will be a change. In the distant heaven there will appear a

"POINT OF LIGHT,"

outshining the sun. It will be seen descending toward the earth. As it descends it will assume the form of a bright cloud, out of which shall stream dazzling beams of light, and flashes of lightning. It will descend apace as if on the wings of the whirlwind, and when it reaches its destination over the brow of the Mt. of Olives it will stop and unfold itself to the terrified and awestricken beholders, and there will be revealed to them Jesus seated on a "White Horse" (Rev. 19:11-16) and accompanied with His Saints and the armies of Heaven. Then shall be fulfilled what Jesus foretold in His Olivet Discourse—"Then shall appear the sign (a cloud) of the Son of Man in heaven; and then shall all the tribes of the earth mourn, and they shall see the Son of Man coming in the **clouds of Heaven WITH POWER AND GREAT GLORY."** Matt. 24:30.

A PRACTICAL DOCTRINE

But why, you ask, should we put so much emphasis on the "Second Coming of Christ"? Why not talk and preach about the practical affairs of life? About the social and commercial problems of the world and their solution through the Gospel? The answer is that the only way to solve these problems is for Christ to return, and the longer His "Return" is delayed, the longer it will be before these problems are solved.

1. AS TO THE JEWS.

The Jews are a downtrodden people. Their only hope is the Return of the Lord. When He comes back they shall be restored to their own land and become a nation again. "Therefore, behold, the days come, saith the Lord, that it shall no more be said, The Lord liveth, that brought up the Children of Israel out of the Land of Egypt; but the Lord liveth that brought up the Children of Israel **from the land of the NORTH** (Russia) **and from ALL THE LANDS** whither He had driven them; and I will bring them again into their **land that I gave unto their fathers."** Jer. 16:14, 15; Isa. 43:5-7. And they shall never again be dispersed. "For I will set mine eyes upon them for good, and I will bring them again to this land; and I will build them, and **not pull them down**; and I will plant them, and **not pluck them up."** Jer. 24:6. This has never as yet been fulfilled.

2. AS TO JERUSALEM AND PALESTINE.

"Thus saith the Lord Jehovah; in the day that I will cleanse you from all your iniquities I will cause the cities (of Palestine) to be inhabited, and the waste places shall be builded. And the land that was desolate shall be tilled. . . . And they shall say, this land that was desolate is become like the garden of Eden." Ez. 36:33-35. Joel 3:18. Joel 2:24-26. "Thus saith the Lord of Hosts; there shall yet old men and old women dwell in the streets of Jerusalem, and every man with his staff in his hand for very age. And the streets of the city shall be full of boys and girls playing in the streets thereof." Zech. 8:4, 5. Zech. 14:20, 21.

3. AS TO THE NATIONS.

When the Lord Jesus Christ returns He will sit upon the "Throne of His Glory" at Jerusalem, and shall separate the "Sheep Nations" from the "Goat Nations," and only the "Sheep Nations" will survive as nations and be permitted to become part of the Millennial Kingdom. Matt. 25:31-40. These nations will become righteous. "And it shall come to pass that every one that is left of all the nations which came against Jerusalem shall even go up from year to year to worship the King, the Lord of Hosts, and to keep the 'Feast of Tabernacles.'" Zech. 14:16. As the result of all this the nations "shall beat their swords into plowshares and their spears into pruning hooks; nation shall not lift up a sword against nation, neither shall they learn war any more. But they shall sit every man under his vine and under his fig tree; and none shall make them afraid." Micah 4:3, 4. Isa. 2:4. The only way then to stop wars and labor troubles and all socialistic and anarchistic movements is for Christ to return and set up His Millennial Kingdom.

4. AS TO SATAN.

The only way to get rid of Satan and all his evil influences and powers is for Christ to come back, for when He comes back Satan will be bound and cast into the Bottomless Pit for 1000 years. Rev. 20:1-3.

5. AS TO THE EARTH.

Since the Fall of Man the earth has been cursed with thorns and thistles and all kind of insect pests and disease germs, and man by the sweat of his face has been compelled to earn his daily bread. Even the brute creation became carnivorous and learned to prey upon each other, and the "whole creation groaneth and travaileth in pain together until now." Rom. 8:22. But all this will be changed when Christ comes back, for then "the wilderness and the solitary place shall be glad for them; and the desert shall rejoice and blossom as the rose." Isa. 5:1. "Then shall the earth yield her increase." Psa. 67:6. And the ploughman will **"overtake the reaper,"** and the treader of grapes him that "soweth seed." Amos 9:13.

THE BLESSED HOPE

The Second Coming of Christ is **"The Blessed Hope."** Writing to Titus Paul said—"Looking for that **'Blessed Hope,'** and the **'Glorious**

Appearing' of the Great God and our Saviour Jesus Christ." **Titus** 2:13. Most Christians when speaking of their "Hope" mean their "Hope of **Salvation,**" but we cannot "hope" for a thing we **have** and salvation is a present possession if we are trusting in Christ as our Saviour. The Christian's "Hope" then is the "Return of His Lord." Man is a three-fold being, he has a **body, a soul,** and a **spirit,** for him to die is to lose his "body." Now he knows that he cannot get his body back until the Resurrection and he also knows that there can be no Resurrection until Christ comes back. Therefore to him Christ's return is "The Blessed Hope," not only that if he dies he will then be raised, but it is to him the "Hope" that Christ will come back **before he dies** and he shall be "caught up" to meet Him **in the air without** dying. I Thess. 4:13-18.

"The Blessed Hope" is also a **"Purifying Hope." "And every man** that hath this hope in him **PURIFIETH HIMSELF." I** John **3:1-3.** That is, every one who is looking for the Lord's return will try to keep himself **pure.** It will make us **"Patient."** "Be **patient** therefore, brethren, unto the **Coming of the Lord.** . . . Be ye also **patient;** stablish your hearts; for the Coming of the Lord draweth nigh." James 5:7, 8. It will make us **"Watchful."** "Watch ye therefore, for ye know not when the Master of the house cometh, at even, or at midnight, or at the cock-crowing, or in the morning; lest coming suddenly he find you sleeping. And what I say unto you I say unto all—**WATCH."** Mark 13:35-37. If we are watching for the Lord we will be careful of our conduct. We will not want Him to come and find us doing questionable things, or in questionable places. We will not want to hoard money, nor spend our money in an extravagant manner, we will want to lay up for ourselves treasures in heaven by contributing to missions. We will see to it that in our homes there is no kind of literature, or art, or pictures, or anything that we would not like His pure eyes to see if He were to be a visitor in our home. In short, "The Blessed Hope" helps us to cling lightly to this world. It will not make us idle and negligent, but will fill us with zeal to be found a faithful servant at His return. For this reason it is a noteworthy fact and a witness to the power of the doctrine, that those who believe it are the most consecrated, unselfish, and strenuous workers in the Master's service.

This "Hope" will also keep us from being **"ASHAMED"** at His Coming. "And now, little children, abide in Him; that when He **shall appear,** we may have confidence, and not be **ASHAMED** before **Him at His Coming."** I John 2:28. If we are watching for Him and our house is in order, and we are ready to give a faithful account of our Stewardship we shall not be ashamed before Him at His coming. Matt. 25:14-30.

The "Hope" of the Lord's Premillennial Return fills the heart of those who believe it with **Joy.** In Luke 24:52 we read that when Jesus was parted from His Disciples and ascended into Heaven, that "They returned to Jerusalem with **GREAT JOY,** and were continually in the Temple, **PRAISING** and **BLESSING** God." That seems strange conduct on their part, for naturally we would suppose that His Departure would have filled them with **sadness.** But when we recall that, when

He Ascended, two men stood by in white apparel and told them that Jesus would come back again, we can understand their **joyfulness.** Acts 1:11.

It has often been said in opposition to the doctrine of the Second Coming, "If Christian people believe that Jesus is soon coming back why do they build houses and churches and make investments and plan for the education of their children and so on?" The answer is that Jesus' coming back will not do away with the need for houses and churches and education. The world moved on just as before after His First Coming, and it will do the same after His Second Coming. People will need homes and churches. Business will go on as before, and the unconverted children of Christian believers will be left behind and need homes and education and means to live on. The prosperity of the world will be greater during the Millennium than ever before. So there is no occasion for those who are looking for the Lord's Return to neglect the affairs of this life. What we as Christians hope for is that the Lord will come back and take us out of the world before the awful days of the "Tribulation Period" come, and then when they are over and Jesus comes back to reign we shall come back with Him as glorified beings to rule and reign over the Millennial earth, and probably visit churches where once we worshipped, and institutions that our money built.

The preacher of the Doctrine of the Premillennial Coming of Christ wields a "two-edged sword." The unbeliever when urged to become a Christian may say I am young and there is plenty of time and so may put off the time of decision, but when he is told that it is not a question of time, or the mere salvation of his **soul,** but that Jesus may be back at any time and it is a question of being ready to meet Him, then he sees the importance of immediate decision.

Dear reader of this pamphlet, are you a Christian, and as a Christian are you a believer in the "Blessed Hope," and are you looking for the speedy coming of the Lord, and doing all you can to hasten His Return, and thus bring back **THE KING?** If not, I beseech you to drop everything and settle the question of whether you will be "caught up" to meet the Lord in the air when He comes, and thus escape the awful days that are coming on the earth—days in which no one can buy or sell unless he has the "Mark of the Beast," and all those who have that "Mark" are eternally doomed. Rev. 13:15-17.

The Transfiguration

A Rehearsal of the Second Coming

Because Jesus said on the day when Peter confessed—"Thou art the Christ, the Son of the Living God" (Matt. 16:13-28), "Verily, I say unto you, There be some **standing here,** which shall not **taste of death, till** they see the Son of Man **COMING IN HIS KINGDOM,"** there are those who contend that the fulfillment of those words required the return of Jesus, and the setting up of the Kingdom during the lifetime of the Disciples, and that therefore because no **literal** Kingdom was set up during the lifetime of the Disciples, Jesus must have meant a **"Spiritual** Kingdom," which they claim was inaugurated on the "Day of Pentecost" and that Jesus now reigns through the Church.

Is this true? If not, what is the explanation of Jesus' words? Here we see the misleading character of the chapter divisions in the King James Version of the Scriptures. There should be no chapter division between Matthew 16th and 17th. The passage should read—

> "Verily I say unto you, There be some **standing here,** which shall not **taste of death,** till they see the Son of Man **COMING IN HIS KINGDOM.** And after six days Jesus taketh Peter, James, and John his brother, and bringeth them up into an high mountain apart, and was **TRANSFIGURED** before them: and His face did **shine as the sun,** and His raiment was **white as the light.** And, behold, there appeared unto them Moses and Elias (Elijah) talking with Him." Matt. 16:28; 17:1-3.

In this "Transfiguration Scene" we have a fulfillment of Jesus' words, that there were **some,** only three, Peter, James, and John, of His Disciples, who should not **"taste of death"** until they saw the Son of Man "Coming in His Kingdom," for the "Transfiguration Scene" was a **"rehearsal"** of the "Second Stage" (Revelation) of Christ's Second Coming. Like as John was transported across the centuries into the "Day of the Lord," and had revealed to him in the Book of Revelation the things that are to come to pass in the "Latter Days," so Peter, James and John had a **"Foreview"** on the Mount of Transfiguration, of the Coming of Christ in His Glory. In that "Scene" Moses was a type of the "First Resurrection Saints" (Jude 9), and Elijah of those who shall be "caught out" without dying (II Kings 2:11); and their glory on the Holy Mount is a sample of the Glory of the Saints at the Rapture. That this is a correct interpretation of Jesus' words is clear from the statement of Peter—

> "For we have not followed cunningly devised fables, when we made known unto you the **power** and **COMING** of our Lord Jesus Christ, but were **eye-witnesses** of His Majesty (Glory). For He received from God the Father **Honor** and **Glory,** when there came such a voice to Him from the **'Excellent Glory.'** This is My Beloved Son, in whom I am well pleased. And this Voice which came from Heaven we **heard, WHEN WE WERE WITH HIM IN THE HOLY MOUNT"** (the Mount of Transfiguration). II Pet. 1:16-18. (Matt. 17:5.)

From the use of the word **"COMING"** in this passage we see that the "Transfiguration Scene" was a "Foreview" of the "Second Coming," and was a fulfillment of Jesus' words that some of His Disciples should not taste of death until they saw the Son of Man **"Coming in His KINGDOM."**

Another passage has been cited in the attempt to prove that the Coming of the Son of Man is only spiritual. It is—

> "But when they persecute you in this city, flee ye into another; for verily I say unto you, Ye shall not have gone **over the cities of Israel,** till the Son of Man **BE COME."** Matt. 10:23.

These words were addressed to the "Twelve Disciples." Jesus sent them forth to preach, that "the Kingdom of Heaven was **AT HAND."** They were limited in their ministry to the **"Lost Sheep of the House of Israel,"** and were forbidden to go to the **Gentiles** or **Samaritans.** Matt. 10:1-7. They never finished their work. The King was rejected, and the offer of the Kingdom at that time was withdrawn, hence the Coming of the Son of Man was postponed. But the Gospel of the Kingdom is to be renewed after the Church is "caught out," and will be preached by the "Two Witnesses" (Moses and Elijah) and the "Godly Remnant" of Israel during the "Tribulation Period," and when they shall, in that day, have gone over the "Cities of Israel," Christ will return to the Mt. of Olives.

The Spirit World

As the purpose of the "First Stage" of Christ's Second Coming is to **reunite** the "Soul" and "Body" of the "Righteous Dead," as well as to "catch out" the "Righteous Living," it will be helpful to have some knowledge of the "Spirit World." We must not forget that man is a **"trinity,"** composed of **"body," "soul,"** and **"spirit"** (I Thess. 5:23. Heb. 4:12), and that the "soul" is the **body** or home of the "spirit" between the death of the physical body and its resurrection, and that our physical or material body corresponds to our "soulish body" as the glove does to the hand that it covers, and that our "soulish body" can **see,** and **hear,** and **feel,** and **think,** and **speak.** As proof of this we have the story of the "Rich Man and Lazarus." Luke 16:19-31. This is not a parable, for parables do not give proper names, as Abraham and Lazarus, but is an account of the state of the Righteous and Wicked in the other world. As we know from the narrative, the **bodies** of both Lazarus and the Rich Man were **buried on the earth.** The account then is descriptive of what happened to them in their **disembodied state** in the "Underworld," and from it we learn that they could **see, hear, feel, thirst, talk,** and **remember,** proving that they had not lost **self consciousness,** and that there is no such thing as **SOUL SLEEP.** We also must not forget that to the Jew "Abraham's Bosom" was a type of "Paradise." "The Underworld" (Hades) in Christ's day was made up of two compartments, "Paradise" and "Hell," separated by an **"impassable gulf."** See the Chart, "The Heavens," page 34, letters **"P," "H,"** and **"K."** "Hell" is the abode of the **souls** of the Wicked between the death and resurrection of their bodies. After the resurrection of their bodies, and their judgment before the "Great White Throne" (W), the Wicked go to the "Lake of Fire" (G). Rev. 20:12-15*

When Jesus died on the Cross His **body** was buried in the tomb of Joseph of Arimathea (Matt. 27:57-60), and His **soul** went to Paradise, where He had an engagement that day to meet the **soul** of the "Penitent Thief" (Luke 23:43), whose **body** was buried in the "Potter's Field." It was in their **"Soulish Bodies"** then that they met in Paradise. When Jesus' **"soul"** returned from "Paradise" on the third day to reoccupy His body in Joseph's tomb, He did not return alone, He led **"captivity captive"** (Eph. 4:8-10) and brought out with Him all the souls of the "Righteous Dead" imprisoned in the Paradise section (P) of the "Underworld," and placed them in the "Paradise" of the "Third Heaven" (E), to which Paul was caught up. II Cor. 12:1-4. This is clear from other scriptures. Jesus said the **"Gates of Hell"** (Hades, the Underworld) should not prevail against the Church. Matt. 16:18. Then "Hell" (Hades) has **gates** to prevent the escape of its inmates. What Jesus did before He came back from the "Un-

---

*For a full account of the "Spirit World" see the writer's book on "The Spirit World." See book notice at the back of this Pamphlet

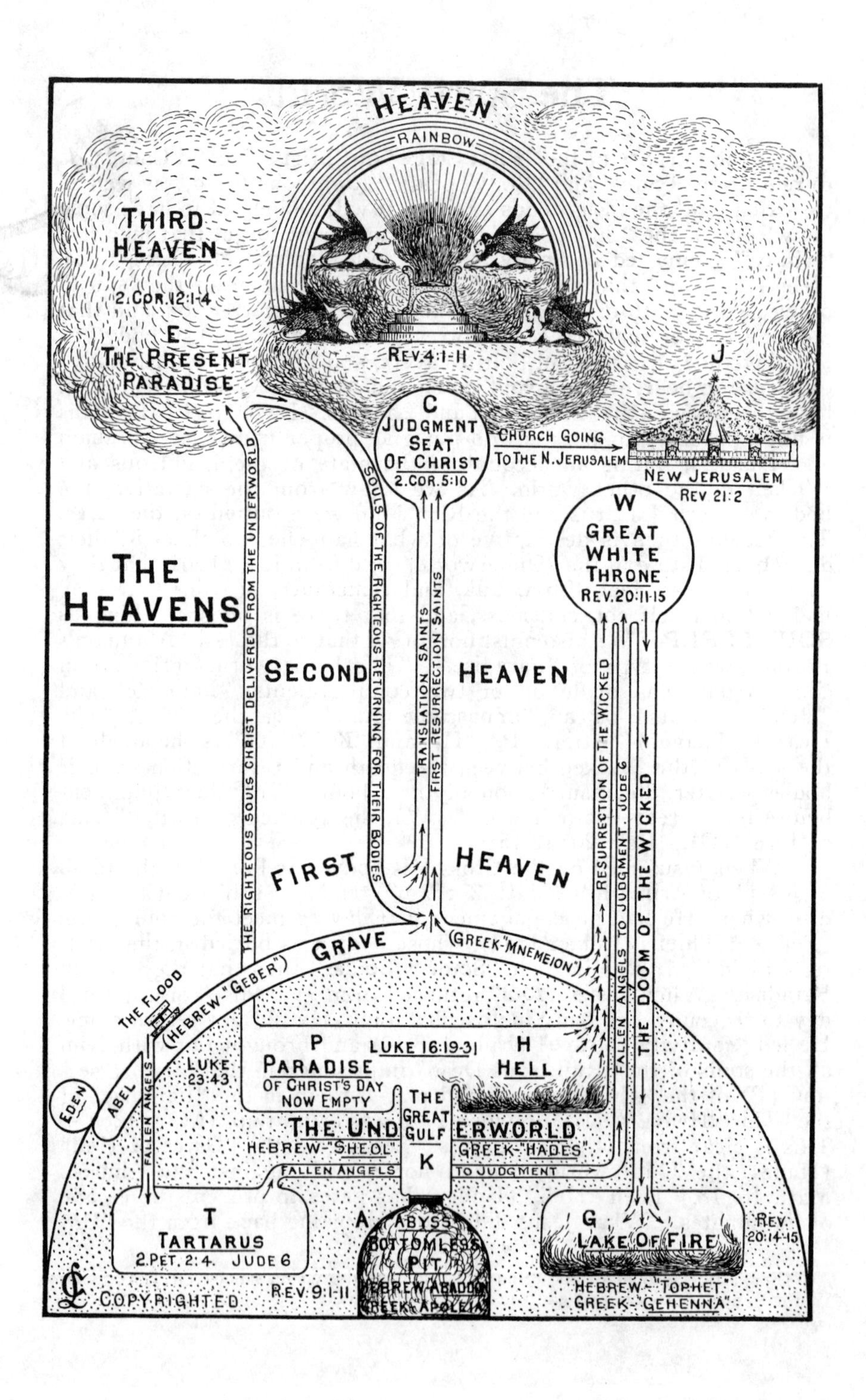
HEAVEN
RAINBOW
THIRD HEAVEN
2 Cor. 12:1-4
E
THE PRESENT PARADISE
Rev. 4:1-11
J
C
JUDGMENT SEAT OF CHRIST
2. Cor. 5:10
CHURCH GOING TO THE N. JERUSALEM
NEW JERUSALEM
REV 21:2
W
GREAT WHITE THRONE
REV. 20:11-15
THE HEAVENS
THE RIGHTEOUS SOULS CHRIST DELIVERED FROM THE UNDERWORLD
SOULS OF THE RIGHTEOUS RETURNING FOR THEIR BODIES
TRANSLATION SAINTS
FIRST RESURRECTION SAINTS
SECOND HEAVEN
RESURRECTION OF THE WICKED
FALLEN ANGELS TO JUDGMENT JUDE 6
THE DOOM OF THE WICKED
FIRST HEAVEN
GRAVE
(HEBREW-"GEBER")
(GREEK-"MNEMEION")
THE FLOOD
EDEN
ABEL
FALLEN ANGELS
LUKE 23:43
P
PARADISE
OF CHRIST'S DAY NOW EMPTY
LUKE 16:19-31
H
HELL
THE GREAT GULF
K
THE UNDERWORLD
HEBREW-"SHEOL"
GREEK-"HADES"
FALLEN ANGELS TO JUDGMENT
T
TARTARUS
2. PET. 2:4. JUDE 6
A
ABYSS
BOTTOMLESS PIT
HEBREW ABADDON
GREEK APOLEIA
REV. 9:1-11
G
LAKE OF FIRE
REV. 20:14-15
HEBREW-"TOPHET"
GREEK-"GEHENNA"
COPYRIGHTED

derworld" was to seize the "Keys of Hades," unlock the **"Gates"** of the "Paradise Section" (P) and empty it of its inmates, and then lock it up that it might remain empty. As proof of this we have Jesus' declaration to John on the Isle of Patmos, 66 years later, when He said—"I am **He** that **liveth,** and **was dead:** and, behold, I am **alive for evermore,** Amen: and have the **'KEYS OF HELL'** (Hades) and of **DEATH** (the Grave)." Rev. 1:18. Jesus then by His Resurrection unlocked not only the "Paradise Section" of "Hades" and transferred the souls of the "Righteous Dead" to the "Paradise Section" of the Third Heaven, but He also has the **"Keys of DEATH,"** that is, of the **"GRAVE,"** and when the time comes He will unlock the graves of the dead and resurrect their bodies. As far as we know the **souls** of the "Wicked Dead" are still in the "Hell Section" of the "Underworld," and will remain there until the "Second Resurrection" at the close of the Millennium, when they will return to the earth and get their bodies, and then go to the "Great White Throne Judgment," from which they will be consigned to the "Lake of Fire." Rev. 20:12-15.

From what has been said we see that the **souls** of the "Righteous Dead," since the resurrection of Jesus, go to the "Paradise" of the "Third Heaven" (E), that they may be **"WITH THE LORD."** Phil. 1:23. II Cor. 5:8. There they will remain until the time comes for the "Rapture of the Church," when they will return with Jesus, and while He tarries in the air (I Thess. 4:17), they will continue on to the earth (see Chart) and re-enter their resurrected and glorified bodies, for we read that when Jesus comes back He will bring with Him the **souls** of those who **"SLEEP IN JESUS."** I Thess. 4:14. The expression, **"Sleep in Jesus,"** has no reference to "Soul Sleep," but is a term applied only to the **bodies** of the "Righteous Dead," and signifies that we are to think of the **bodies** of the "Dead in Christ" as only sleeping or resting.

While "Paradise," as a suburb of Heaven, is a glorious place, it does not follow that the state of the Righteous there is more blissful than it was in the "Paradise Section" of the Underworld. We must not forget that while the **souls** of the Righteous in Paradise are free from sorrow and sickness, and enjoy the society of the saints of all ages, their state is more one of rest and **waiting** than of activity or service (Rev. 6:9-11), for it is a state of **limitation** and **incompleteness,** for they have not as yet received their resurrection body with all its glorious powers, nor been judged so as to receive their reward, or crown, if they are entitled to any. The description of Heaven and the New Jerusalem as given in the Book of Revelation is still **future,** and the things there described will not come to pass until after the Rapture of the Church. From this we see the meaning of the Apostle when he says—"We groan within ourselves, waiting for the **adoption,** to wit, the **REDEMPTION OF OUR BODY"** (Rom. 8:18-23); and as this is not possible until the Return of the Lord Jesus, who will then change our **"vile body,"** that it may be fashioned like unto His **GLORIOUS BODY"** (Phil. 3:20-21), we should be doing all we can to hasten His Return.

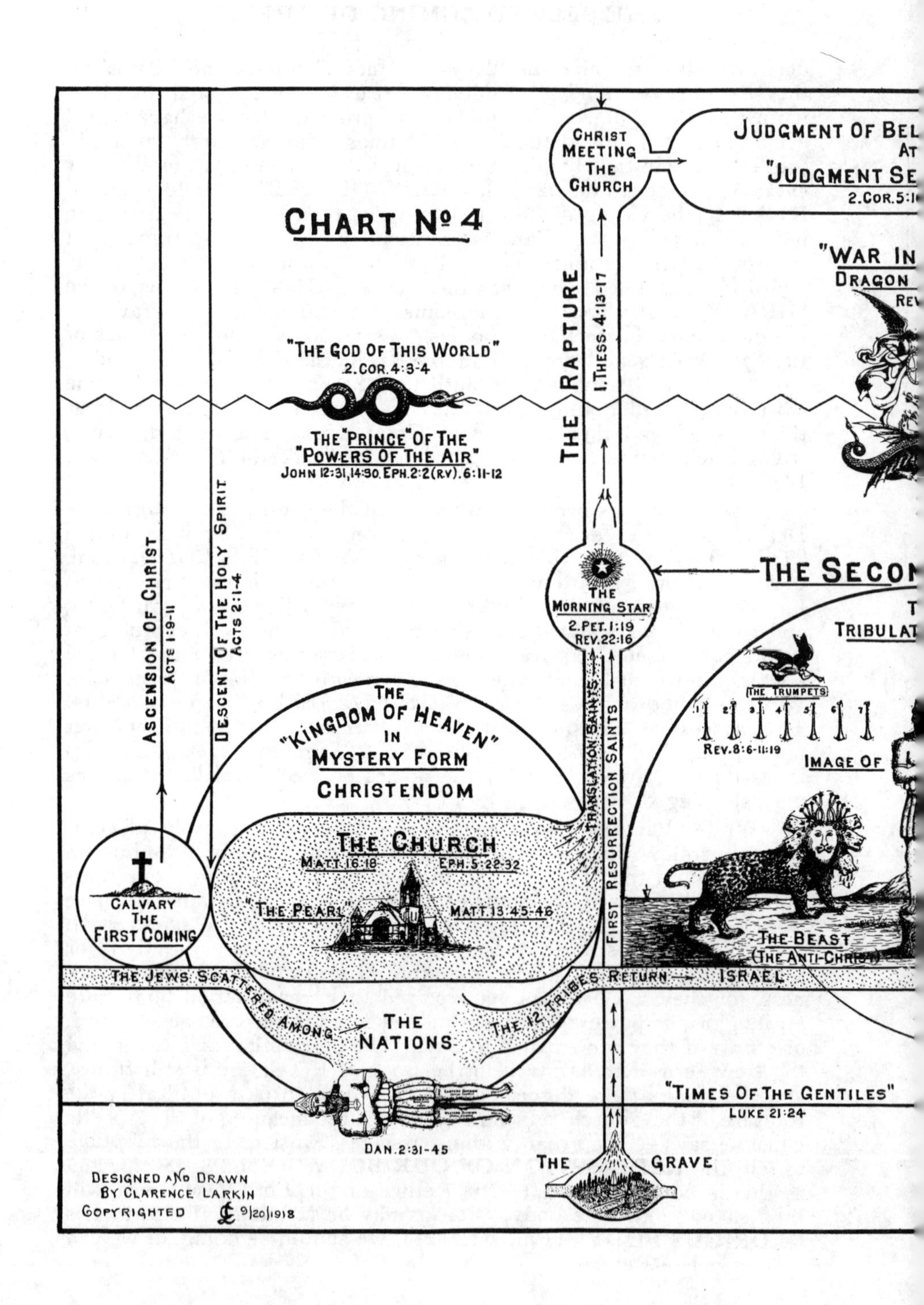
CHART Nº 4
CHRIST MEETING THE CHURCH
JUDGMENT OF BEL
AT
"JUDGMENT SE
2.COR.5:1
"WAR IN
DRAGON
REV
THE RAPTURE
I.THESS.4:13-17
"THE GOD OF THIS WORLD"
2.COR.4:3-4
THE "PRINCE" OF THE "POWERS OF THE AIR"
JOHN 12:31, 14:30. EPH.2:2 (RV). 6:11-12
ASCENSION OF CHRIST
ACTS 1:9-11
DESCENT OF THE HOLY SPIRIT
ACTS 2:1-4
THE MORNING STAR
2.PET.1:19
REV.22:16
THE SECON
T
TRIBULAT
THE TRUMPETS
REV.8:6-11:19
IMAGE OF
THE "KINGDOM OF HEAVEN" IN MYSTERY FORM
CHRISTENDOM
TRANSLATION SAINTS
FIRST RESURRECTION SAINTS
THE CHURCH
MATT.16:18
EPH.5:22-32
"THE PEARL"
MATT.13:45-46
CALVARY
THE
FIRST COMING
THE BEAST
(THE ANTI-CHRIST)
THE JEWS SCATTERED AMONG THE NATIONS
THE 12 TRIBES RETURN
ISRAEL
"TIMES OF THE GENTILES"
LUKE 21:24
DAN.2:31-45
THE GRAVE
DESIGNED AND DRAWN
BY CLARENCE LARKIN
COPYRIGHTED 9/20/1918

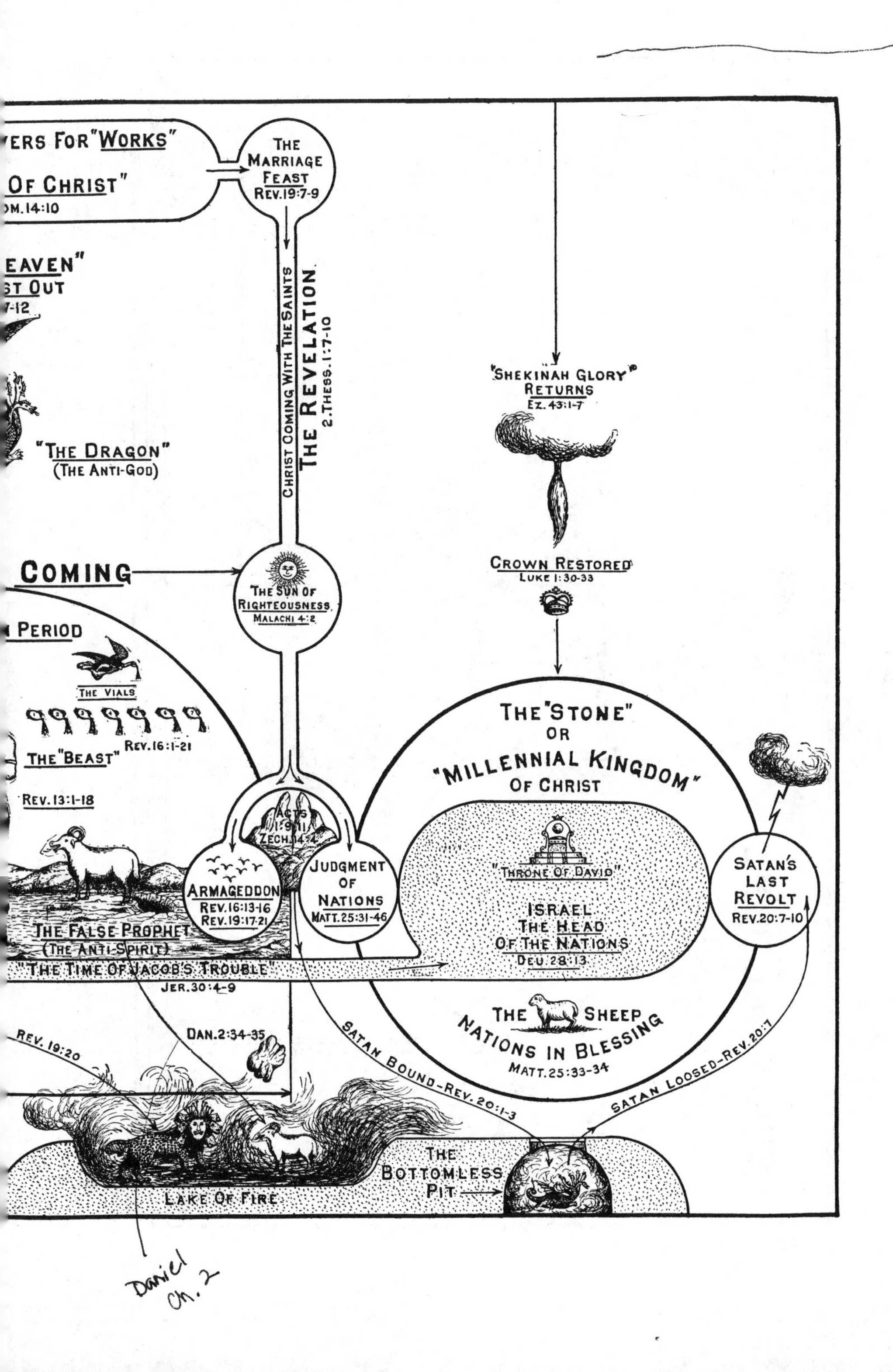

ERS FOR "WORKS"
OF CHRIST"
OM.14:10
THE MARRIAGE FEAST
REV.19:7-9
EAVEN"
ST OUT
7-12
"THE DRAGON"
(THE ANTI-GOD)
CHRIST COMING WITH THE SAINTS
THE REVELATION
2.THESS.1:7-10
"SHEKINAH GLORY"
RETURNS
EZ.43:1-7
COMING
THE SUN OF RIGHTEOUSNESS
MALACHI 4:2
CROWN RESTORED
LUKE 1:30-33
PERIOD
THE VIALS
REV.16:1-21
THE "BEAST"
REV.13:1-18
THE "STONE"
OR
"MILLENNIAL KINGDOM"
OF CHRIST
ACTS 1:9-11
ZECH.14:4
ARMAGEDDON
REV.16:13-16
REV.19:17-21
JUDGMENT OF NATIONS
MATT.25:31-46
"THRONE OF DAVID"
ISRAEL
THE HEAD
OF THE NATIONS
DEU.28:13
SATAN'S LAST REVOLT
REV.20:7-10
THE FALSE PROPHET
(THE ANTI-SPIRIT)
"THE TIME OF JACOB'S TROUBLE"
JER.30:4-9
THE SHEEP
NATIONS IN BLESSING
MATT.25:33-34
REV.19:20
DAN.2:34-35
SATAN BOUND-REV.20:1-3
SATAN LOOSED-REV.20:7
THE BOTTOMLESS PIT
LAKE OF FIRE
Daniel Ch. 2

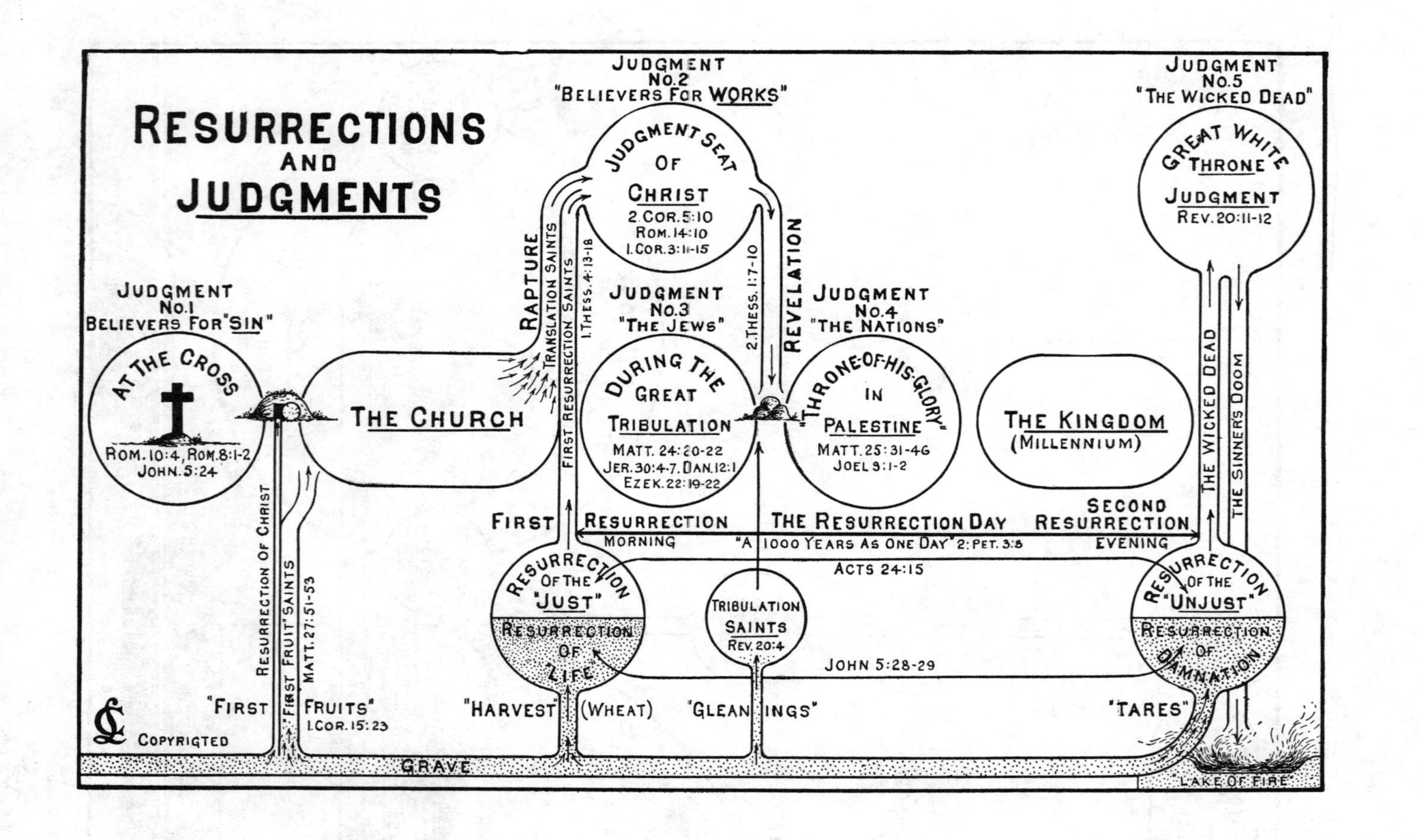
RESURRECTIONS
AND
JUDGMENTS
JUDGMENT
No.1
BELIEVERS FOR "SIN"
AT THE CROSS
ROM. 10:4, ROM. 8:1-2
JOHN. 5:24
RESURRECTION OF CHRIST
FIRST FRUIT SAINTS
MATT. 27:51-53
THE CHURCH
RAPTURE
TRANSLATION SAINTS
FIRST RESURRECTION SAINTS
I. THESS. 4:13-18
JUDGMENT
No.2
"BELIEVERS FOR WORKS"
JUDGMENT SEAT
OF
CHRIST
2. COR. 5:10
ROM. 14:10
I. COR. 3:11-15
2. THESS. 1:7-10
REVELATION
JUDGMENT
No.3
"THE JEWS"
DURING THE
GREAT
TRIBULATION
MATT. 24:20-22
JER. 30:4-7. DAN. 12:1
EZEK. 22:19-22
JUDGMENT
No.4
"THE NATIONS"
"THRONE-OF-HIS-GLORY"
IN
PALESTINE
MATT. 25:31-46
JOEL 3:1-2
THE KINGDOM
(MILLENNIUM)
JUDGMENT
No.5
"THE WICKED DEAD"
GREAT WHITE
THRONE
JUDGMENT
REV. 20:11-12
THE WICKED DEAD
THE SINNER'S DOOM
FIRST RESURRECTION
MORNING
THE RESURRECTION DAY
"A 1000 YEARS AS ONE DAY" 2: PET. 3:8
SECOND
RESURRECTION
EVENING
ACTS 24:15
RESURRECTION
OF THE
"JUST"
RESURRECTION
OF
LIFE
TRIBULATION
SAINTS
REV. 20:4
JOHN 5:28-29
RESURRECTION
OF THE
"UNJUST"
RESURRECTION
OF
DAMNATION
"FIRST FRUITS"
I. COR. 15:23
"HARVEST" (WHEAT)
"GLEANINGS"
"TARES"
COPYRIGTED
GRAVE
LAKE OF FIRE

The Resurrections

The Scriptures speak of "Two Resurrections." One of the **"JUST"** (the Justified, or Righteous), the other of the **"UNJUST"** (the Unjustified, or Wicked). Acts 24:15. The character of these Resurrections is different, for one is unto **"LIFE"** (Eternal Life), the other is unto **"DAMNATION"** (Eternal Punishment). John 5:28-29. The **"Time Space"** between these Resurrections is **1000 years,** and they are designated as the **"First"** and **"Second"** Resurrections. Rev. 20:4-6. As a **"day"** with the Lord is as a **"1000 years"** (II Pet. 3:8), and the Millennium is a 1000 years long, then the **"FIRST"** Resurrection (that of the Righteous) will take place on the **Morning** of the "Millennial Day," and the **"SECOND"** Resurrection (that of the Wicked) as the **Evening Shadows Fall.** In this Pamphlet we are only interested in the resurrection of the Righteous.* The Apostle Paul gives us an account of it in I Cor. 15:35-49. In verses 50-55 he describes the transformation of the "Living Saints" as simultaneous with the resurrection of the Dead in Christ. (1) The Apostle tells us that this **"vile body"** is sown in **"Corruption,"** that is, in **"foul rottenness"** so offensive that we are compelled to box up the remains of our loved ones and bury them in the earth, but that it is to be raised in **"INCORRUPTION."** (2) It is sown in **"Dishonor,"** caused by sin, but shall be raised in **"GLORY."** That is it shall be fashioned like unto His—**"GLORIOUS BODY."** Phil. 3:20-21. (3) It is sown in **"Weakness."** How weak is the body ravaged by disease, but it shall be raised in **"POWER."** Not only will God manifest His power in raising the dead, but those raised shall have physical powers far surpassing any that they have now. They shall have **"X-Ray"** power of sight, **"Megaphone"** power of speech, **"Wireless"** power of communication, **"Telephonic"** power of hearing, and **"Aeronautic"** power of flight through the ether, that shall enable them to traverse the highways and byways of the "Stellar Spaces," and pass from Heaven to earth as a beam of light. (4) It is sown a **"Natural** Body," it is raised a **"SPIRITUAL** Body." By **"Spiritual"** body we are not to understand some sort of **"Etherealized Ghost-like Structure"** that has no substance. Every **"Force"** in the Universe must have a **"Motor,"** that is a **machine** adapted to its use. The motive force of the human body is the **"Soul,"** and of the "Resurrection Body" the **"SPIRIT."** "The 'First Adam' was made a **'Living Soul'**; the 'Last Adam' a **'QUICKENING SPIRIT'."** I Cor. 15:45. From this we see that our "Resurrection Body" is called a **"SPIRITUAL"** body because its "motive force" will be that of **"SPIRIT,"** not the Holy Spirit, but the **"Spirit Power"** that runs the Universe. Nevertheless, it will be a **Material body,** not a **"Will o' the Wisp,"** but of **"flesh"** (spirit flesh) and **"bones"** such as Jesus' Resurrection body had. Luke 24:36-39. O happy day, when the undressed soul shall put on the fadeless beauty and undying glory of the "Resurrection Body." That will be the Easter of all Easters, when the voice of the Archangel shall summon the sainted dead to rise, and corruption shall put on incorruption, and we shall be caught up to meet the Lord in the Air. I Thess. 4:13-18.

*For a fuller description of the Resurrections see the writer's book on "The Spirit World."

The Imminency of the Second Coming

One of the objections to the Doctrine of the "Second Coming of Christ" is the claim that He may come back at any time. Post-millennialists tell us that the writers of the New Testament looked for Him to come back in their day, and as He did not do so, is proof that they were mistaken, and that Paul in his later writings modified his statements as to the imminency of Christ's return. It is a fact that while Jesus said: "Watch therefore: for ye know not **what hour** your Lord doth come. . . . Therefore be ye also ready: for in such an hour **as ye think not** the Son of man cometh" (Matt. 24:42-44), He did not in these passages teach that He would return during the **lifetime** of those who listened to Him. In fact, in His Parables He intimated that His return would be delayed, as in the Parable of The Talents, where it is said: "After a **long time** the Lord of those servants cometh." Matt. 25:19. What Jesus wanted to teach was the sudden and unexpected character of His return. As to the Apostles, while they exhorted their followers to be ready, for the "night is **far spent,** the day **is at hand,"** and the "coming of the Lord **draweth nigh,"** their language simply implied **"imminency,"** but not necessarily **"IMMEDIATENESS."** And the use of the word **"WE"** in I Cor. 15:51, **"WE"** shall not all **sleep,** but **WE** shall all be **changed,"** is not a declaration that the Lord would return in Paul's day and some would not die but be translated, for the Apostle is talking about the Rapture and he means by **"We"** a certain class of persons, the saints that shall be alive when that event occurs, whether in his day or at some later time.

It was clearly known to our Lord that certain events must come to pass before His Return, but to have disclosed that fact would have nullified the command to **"Watch,"** therefore He in **"mystery form,"** as in the seven parables of Matt. 13, hid the fact that His Return would be delayed. It would take time for the "Sowing of the Seed," the growth of the "Wheat" and "Tares," the growth of the "Mustard Tree," and the "Leavening of the Meal." So rapid was the spread of the Gospel in the first century that the followers of Christ were warranted in looking for the speedy Return of the Lord, but it was true then, as in every century since, that we do not know what the extent of the "Harvest" is to be, and when it will be ripe, so the Lord can return. Matt. 13:30. Uncertainty then as to the **"time"** of the Lord's return is necessary to promote the **"watchful"** spirit. If the early Church had known that the Lord's Return would have been delayed for **20** centuries, the incentive to watchfulness would have been wanting.

By **"Imminency"** we mean **"may happen at any time."** For illustration, you hurry to the railroad station to catch a train. You find the train has not arrived, though it is past the hour. Though it is late it is on the way, and it would not be safe for you to leave the station, for it may arrive any minute, but as a **matter of fact,**

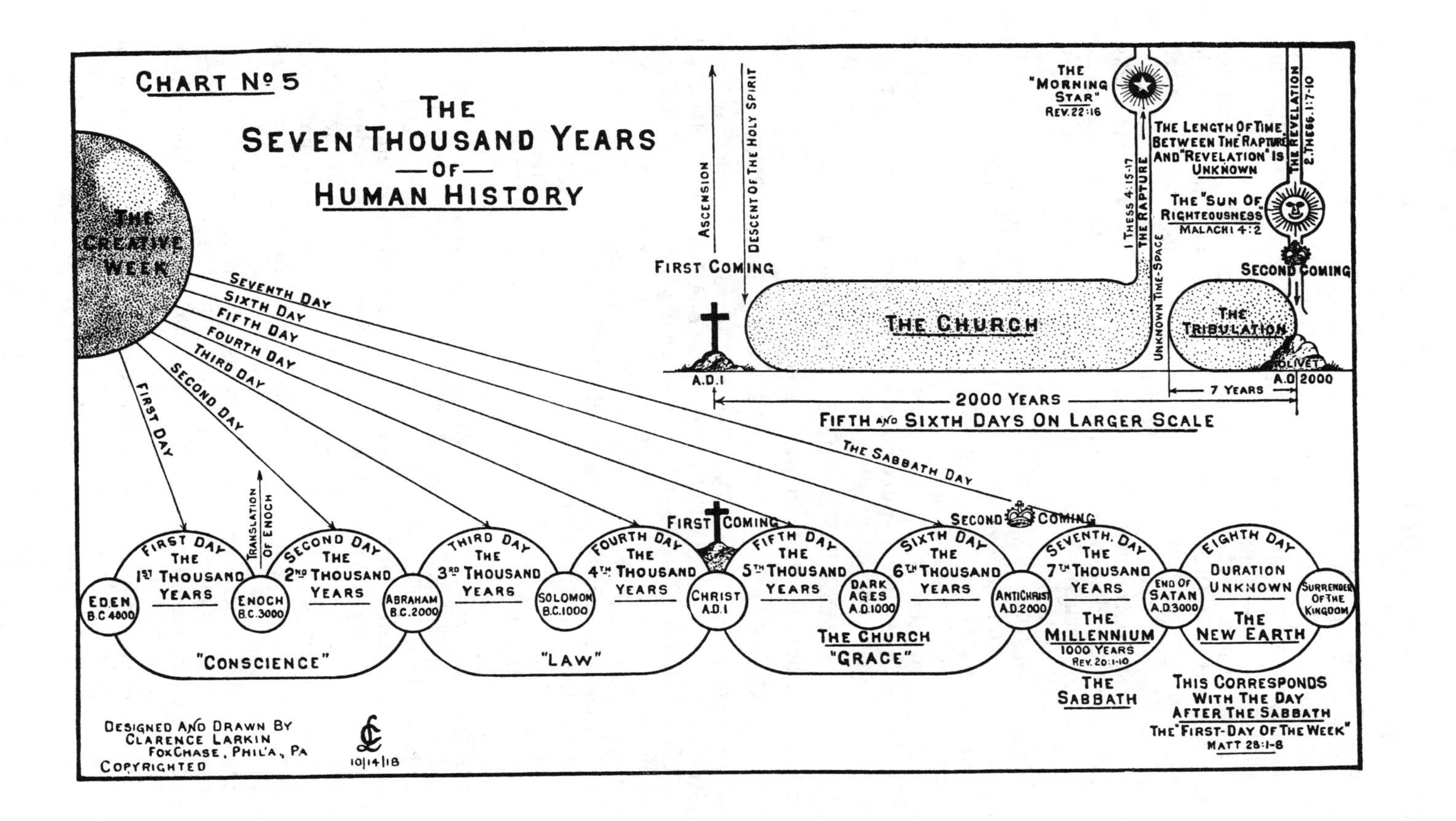

Chart No 5
The Seven Thousand Years of Human History
The Creative Week
Seventh Day
Sixth Day
Fifth Day
Fourth Day
Third Day
Second Day
First Day
Ascension
Descent of the Holy Spirit
First Coming
A.D. 1
The Church
The "Morning Star" Rev. 22:16
1 Thess 4:15-17 The Rapture
Unknown Time-Space
The Length of Time Between the Rapture and "Revelation" Is Unknown
The Revelation 2 Thess. 1:7-10
The "Sun of Righteousness" Malachi 4:2
Second Coming
The Tribulation
Olivet
A.D. 2000
7 Years
2000 Years
Fifth and Sixth Days on Larger Scale
The Sabbath Day
Translation of Enoch
Eden B.C. 4000
First Day The 1st Thousand Years
Enoch B.C. 3000
Second Day The 2nd Thousand Years
"Conscience"
Abraham B.C. 2000
Third Day The 3rd Thousand Years
Solomon B.C. 1000
Fourth Day The 4th Thousand Years
"Law"
First Coming
Christ A.D. 1
Fifth Day The 5th Thousand Years
Dark Ages A.D. 1000
Sixth Day The 6th Thousand Years
The Church "Grace"
Second Coming
AntiChrist A.D. 2000
Seventh Day The 7th Thousand Years
The Millennium 1000 Years Rev. 20:1-10
The Sabbath
End of Satan A.D. 3000
Eighth Day Duration Unknown
The New Earth
Surrender of the Kingdom
This Corresponds With the Day After the Sabbath The "First-Day of the Week" Matt 28:1-8
Designed and Drawn By Clarence Larkin Fox Chase, Phil'a, Pa
Copyrighted
10/14/18

it does not come for half an hour. Now if you had known that it would not arrive for half an hour you would have used the time in some other way than **"waiting"** and **"watching."** So we see that **"Imminency"** does not necessarily imply **"IMMEDIATENESS,"** but does demand **"Watchfulness."**

It is the firm conviction of the writer that there has been **unnecessary delay** in the Return of the Lord, caused by the failure of the Church to obey the "Divine Commission" to evangelize the world (Matt. 28:19, 20), and it is past the time when He should have returned. Of course, this was **foreseen** by God, and His **foreknowledge has held** back the development of the forces of evil, etc., until the "Fulness of the Gentiles" should be gathered in, and the "Harvest" is ripe for the gathering. Rev. 14:14-20. At no time in the history of the Christian Church have the conditions necessary to the Lord's Return been so completely fulfilled as at the present time; therefore, His Coming is **IMMINENT,** and will not probably be long delayed. Let us be ready and watching.

While the writer, as stated, is disposed to believe that the Return of the Lord is "past due," and while he is no "time setter," yet there is a "theory" that may throw some light on the

IMMINENCY OF HIS RETURN

that it might be well to examine. It is called

THE GREAT WEEK OF HUMAN HISTORY,

and is based on the **"Seven Days"** of the **"Creative Week,"** and the declaration of scripture (II Pet. 3:8), "That **one day** is with the Lord as a **THOUSAND YEARS,** and a **thousand years** as **ONE DAY."** The Millennium in the Old Testament is described as a "Sabbath Keeping" period of rest, and is referred to as such in Heb. 4:4-11, where it is associated with the **"Seventh Day"** of the "Creative Week." Now we know that the length of the Millennium is **1000 YEARS** (Rev. 20:1-9), and if it corresponds with the "Seventh Day" of the "Creative Week," why should not the remaining **six days** be of the same length? If so, and those days correspond with the past of human history, then from the date of the "Creative Week" up to the beginning of the Millennium should be **6000** years of human history. In confirmation of this we have the **fact** that a careful study of the genealogical tables and history of the Old Testament seem to show that from Adam to Christ was about **4000 years,** or **four days** of a thousand years each, corresponding to the first four days of the "Creative Week," and from Christ down to the present time we have over **1900** years, or nearly 2 days of **1000 years each,** thus making nearly **6 days** of **1000 years each** of human history, and as Christ is to come back **before** the Millennium, and all signs point to His speedy return, then the "theory" that the "Seven Days" of the "Creative Week" are typical of Seven "One Thousand Year Periods" is not unwarranted in Scripture.

If our inference is correct, then it follows that the Return of the Lord will take place before the close of this present century. How much before is uncertain. If the Millennium is to be ushered in in A.D. 2000, then the "Rapture" must take place **at least 7 years before that.** See Chart No. 5, on "The Seven Thousand Years of Human History." But right here we must sound a note of caution. There is too much confusion in Biblical Chronology to fix any dates with certainty. Doubtless God has ordered it so, so as to keep us in doubt as to the exact date of the Lord's Return. It may have been 4075 years, instead of 4004 (as generally given), from Adam to Christ. In that case we are living in the year 5993 from the creation of Adam, or on the eve of the Rapture. Again we must not forget that God uses in "Prophetical Chronology" the Calendar Year of 360 days to a year, while we use the Julian or Astronomical Year of 365¼ days, and it would be necessary for us to find out what kind of year is used and reduce it to the Calendar year. Thus we might find that we are nearer the end of the six thousandth year than we are aware, and that the Return of the Lord is **IMMINENT.** However, while we may look upon the above theory as suggestive and in a way confirmatory of the near coming of the Lord, it is not conclusive, and we are not warranted in fixing any date based upon it. And further, we must not forget that the "Rapture" may take place **some time** before the "Tribulation Period" begins and Antichrist is revealed. So if we could fix the exact date when this century will close, and count back 7 years, the Rapture might occur 5, 10 or even 25 years before that, so as to give time for the rebuilding of Babylon and other events that are to occur before the Tribulation Period can begin, otherwise the Rapture would not be a surprise. It is not for the Christian to look for "Times" and "Seasons" and "Signs." To do so will put him in the class of those who say: "My Lord **delayeth His Coming"** (Luke 12:42-48). and he will become preoccupied with other things and neglect to be watchful. Let us live as if we expected the Return of our Lord at any moment.

Two Women Grinding at the Mill.
Luke 17: 30-37.

The History of the Doctrine

The Apostolic Church was Pre-Millennial, and for over 200 years no other view was entertained. The writings of the "Church Fathers" abound in evidence of that fact. But about A. D. 250, Origen, one of the Church Fathers, conceived the idea that the words of Scripture were but the "husk" in which was hid the "kernel" of Scripture truth. At once he began to "Allegorize" and "Spiritualize" the Scriptures, and thus founded that school of "Allegorizing" and "Spiritualizing" interpreters of Scripture, from which the Church and the Bible have suffered so much. The result was that the Church largely ceased to look for the Lord's Return.

When Constantine became sole Emperor of Rome in A. D. 323, he united Church and State, and bestowed such great gifts and privileges on the Church, that it claimed that the Millennial blessings of the Old Testament had been transferred from the Jews to the Christian Church. The arrogance and persecution of the Papal Church led to the charge that it was the "Beast" (Antichrist) of the Book of Revelation. This led to an effort to expunge the Book of Revelation from the Sacred Canon, and when this failed, the Bible was locked up and became a sealed book, and the gloom of night settled down upon all Christendom. The result was the "Dark Ages." But amid the gloom God was not without witnesses to the Blessed Hope. At the Reformation the doctrine of the Premillennial Return of the Lord was revived, but was again lost sight of in the religious controversies that led to the formation of numerous sects. The result was an ebb of spirituality and the growth of Rationalism, which refused to believe that the world was fast ripening for judgment, and a new interpretation of the Millennial Reign of Christ was demanded. This interpretation was furnished by the Rev. Daniel Whitby (1636-1726), a clergyman of the Church of England, who claimed that in reading the promises made to the Jews in the Old Testament of their restoration as a nation, and the re-establishment of the Throne of David, he was led to see that these promises were spiritual and applied to the Church. This view he called a "New Hypothesis."

He claimed that Israel and Mount Zion represented the Church. That the promised submission of the Gentiles to the Jews was simply prophetic of the conversion of the Gentiles and their entrance into the Church. That the lying down of the lion and the lamb together typified the reconciliation of the Old and New natures, and that the establishment of an outward and visible kingdom at Jerusalem, over which Christ and the saints should reign, was gross and carnal, and contrary to reason, as it implied the mingling together of human and spiritual beings on the earth.

His "New Hypothesis" was that by the preaching of the Gospel Mohammedanism would be overthrown, the Jews converted, the Papal Church with the Pope (Antichrist) would be destroyed, and there would follow a 1000 years of righteousness and peace known as the Millennium; at the close of which there would be a short period of Apostasy, ending in the return of Christ. There would then be a general resurrection of the dead, followed by a general judgment, the earth would be destroyed by fire and eternity would begin.

The times were favorable for the "New Theory." A reaction had set in from the open infidelity of those days. All England was in a religious fervor. The "Great Awakening" followed under Whitefield and Wesley, and it looked, as Whitby claimed, that the Millennium was about to be ushered in. That he was mistaken the events of history since that time have shown. It is evident that we are not in the Millennium now, as the "Godless Civilization" of today proves.

Nevertheless his "Theory" was favorably received everywhere, and spread with great rapidity and became an established doctrine of the Church, and is what is known today as the "Post-Millennial" view of the Second Coming of Christ, and supposed to be the orthodox faith of the Church. In short, "Post-Millennialism," as advocated in our day, is barely 200 years old, while "Pre-Millennialism" dates back to the days of Isaiah and Daniel.

The sad thing is that this "false doctrine" of "Post-Millennialism" is taught in our Bibles by the headings of the chapters in the Old Testament. For illustration the headings of chapters forty-three and four of Isaiah read—"The Lord comforteth **The Church** with His promises," whereas the chapters are not addressed to the Church at all, but to **Jacob** and **Israel,** as we see by reading them. The ordinary reader overlooks the fact that the chapter headings of the Bible are put there by the publisher and should be omitted, as they are misleading, as for illustration the title to the Book of Revelation, which is called—

"The Revelation of **St. John the Divine,"** whereas it should be called—

"THE REVELATION OF JESUS CHRIST."
Rev. 1:1.

The fact is, the doctrine of the Premillennial Coming of the Lord is but the revival of the belief of the Apostolic Church that looked for the Return of the Lord at any time.

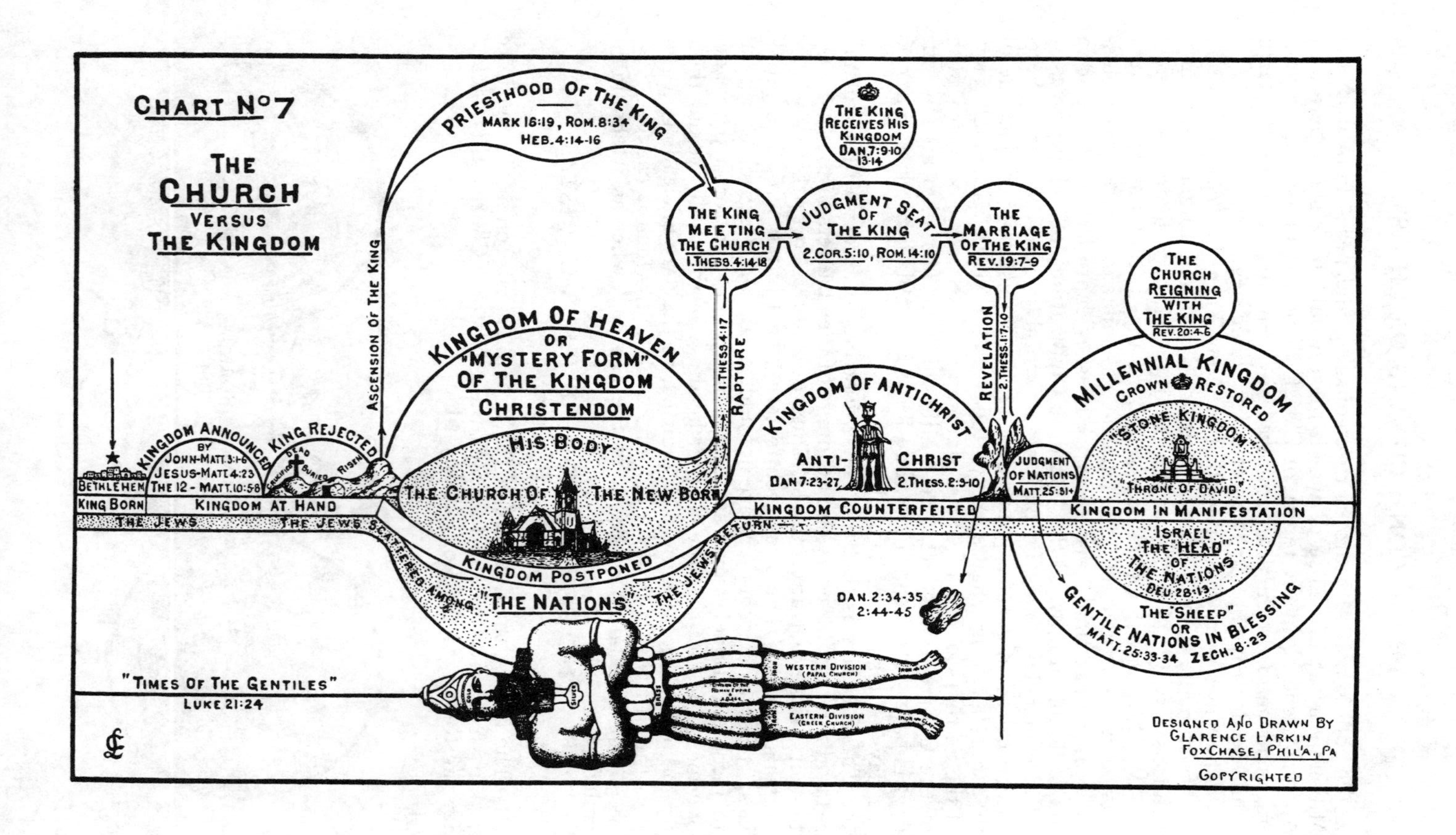
CHART Nº7
THE CHURCH VERSUS THE KINGDOM
PRIESTHOOD OF THE KING
MARK 16:19, ROM. 8:34
HEB. 4:14-16
THE KING RECEIVES HIS KINGDOM
DAN. 7:9-10 13-14
THE KING MEETING THE CHURCH
1. THESS. 4:14-18
JUDGMENT SEAT OF THE KING
2. COR. 5:10, ROM. 14:10
THE MARRIAGE OF THE KING
REV. 19:7-9
THE CHURCH REIGNING WITH THE KING
REV. 20:4-6
ASCENSION OF THE KING
KINGDOM OF HEAVEN OR "MYSTERY FORM" OF THE KINGDOM
CHRISTENDOM
HIS BODY
THE CHURCH OF THE NEW BORN
1. THESS. 4:17
RAPTURE
REVELATION
2. THESS. 1:7-10
KINGDOM OF ANTICHRIST
ANTI- CHRIST
DAN 7:23-27
2. THESS. 2:3-10
MILLENNIAL KINGDOM
CROWN RESTORED
"STONE KINGDOM"
"THRONE OF DAVID"
JUDGMENT OF NATIONS
MATT. 25:31+
KINGDOM ANNOUNCED
BY
JOHN-MATT. 3:1-6
JESUS-MATT. 4:23
THE 12 - MATT. 10:5-8
KING REJECTED
CRUCIFIED
DEAD
BURIED
RISEN
BETHLEHEM
KING BORN
KINGDOM AT HAND
KINGDOM COUNTERFEITED
KINGDOM IN MANIFESTATION
THE JEWS
THE JEWS SCATTERED AMONG "THE NATIONS"
KINGDOM POSTPONED
THE JEWS RETURN
ISRAEL THE "HEAD" OF THE NATIONS
DEU. 28:13
THE "SHEEP" OR GENTILE NATIONS IN BLESSING
MATT. 25:33-34 ZECH. 8:23
DAN. 2:34-35
2:44-45
"TIMES OF THE GENTILES"
LUKE 21:24
GOLD
SILVER
BRASS
IRON
WESTERN DIVISION (PAPAL CHURCH)
EASTERN DIVISION (GREEK CHURCH)
DESIGNED AND DRAWN BY
CLARENCE LARKIN
FOX CHASE, PHIL'A., PA
COPYRIGHTED

The Church Versus The Kingdom

The "Church" and the "Kingdom" are not identical. They are never confounded in the Scriptures. The Church is compared to a **"House"** (I Tim. 3: 15), to a **"Temple"** (I Cor. 3: 16-17), to a **"Body"** (I Cor. 12: 12-31), but never to a "Kingdom." Christ is the **"HEAD"** of the Church (Eph. 1: 22; 4: 15; 5: 23; Col. 1: 18), but He is never spoken of as its **"KING."** His relation to the Church is that of **"LORD"** (Master). I Tim. 6: 13-14. The saints are not His **"subjects"** or His **"servants,"** they are **fellow "HEIRS."** Rom. 8: 17. The Church is not to be ruled over by Christ, but to rule **with** Him. The Church is **here,** the Kingdom is **TO COME.** The Church is being **"built up,"** a gradual process, the Kingdom is to be **"SET UP,"** a sudden event. The Church is an invisible and Heavenly **"SPIRITUAL ORGANISM,"** entered by the "New Birth," and is to be **"caught out,"** while the Kingdom is an outward, visible, and earthly **"POLITICAL ORGANIZATION"** that is to be **"set up"** on the **EARTH,** of which the Jewish Nation will be the "Head" (Deu. 28: 11-13), and will have a King, a Throne, and a Capital City—Jerusalem. The Kingdom is characterized by a **"Throne,"** the Church by a **"Table."** Thus we see that the Church and the Kingdom have different **"spheres"** of work, and different **"time periods"** in which to do that work. Therefore what God has separated let no man join together.

There is much confusion as to the difference between the **"Kingdom of God,"** the **"Kingdom of Heaven,"** and the **"Church."** No amount of sophistical argument can make them synonymous. The **"KINGDOM OF GOD"** is the all inclusive Kingdom, or rule of the Triune God (Father, Son, and Holy Spirit) over the whole Universe, especially over all moral intelligences, angelic or human, and includes "Time" and "Eternity," "Heaven" and "Hell." It is **SPIRITUAL,** and **"cometh not with observation"** (outward show). Luke 17: 20-21. It is entered by the **"New Birth"** (John 3: 5), and is not **"meat"** and **"drink,"** but **"Righteousness"** and **"Peace,"** and **"Joy"** in the **HOLY GHOST.** Rom. 14: 17. See Chart page 48. The **"KINGDOM OF HEAVEN"** is a New Testament term, and is found in Matthew's Gospel only, where it is mentioned 27 times. It is the earthly sphere of the "Kingdom of God," and is outward and visible. Its character is described in the 12 "Kingdom of Heaven Parables" given in Matt. 13: 1-50; 18: 23-35; 20: 1-16; 22: 1-14; 25: 1-30. From these Parables we see that the "Kingdom of Heaven" is limited as to its **"Time"** and **"Sphere."** Its "Time" is from the First to the Second Coming of Christ, and its "Sphere" is over that part of the world that we call Christendom. In it there is a mixture of **"Good"** and **"Evil,"** of **"Wheat"** and **"Tares,"** of **"Wise Virgins"** and **"Foolish Virgins,"** of **"Good Fish"** and **"Bad Fish."** Entrance into it may be obtained by a righteousness that barely exceeds the righteousness of the Scribes and Pharisees. Dropping the Kingdom, let us now look at the Church.

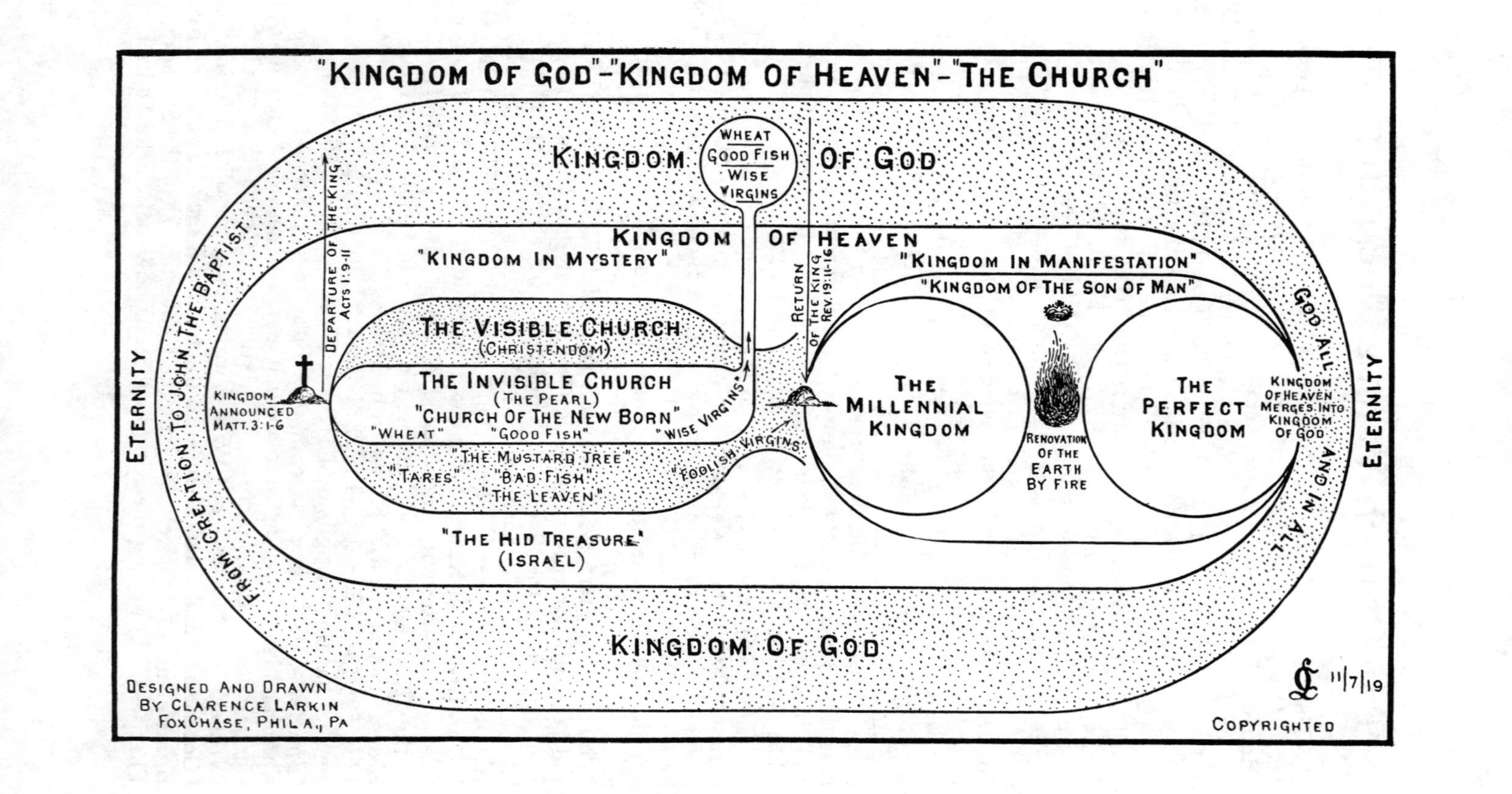
"Kingdom Of God" - "Kingdom Of Heaven" - "The Church"
Kingdom Of God
Wheat
Good Fish
Wise
Virgins
Kingdom Of Heaven
"Kingdom In Mystery"
"Kingdom In Manifestation"
"Kingdom Of The Son Of Man"
Departure Of The King
Acts 1:9-11
Return Of The King
Rev. 19:11-16
The Visible Church
(Christendom)
The Invisible Church
(The Pearl)
"Church Of The New Born"
"Wheat"
"Good Fish"
"Wise Virgins"
"Foolish Virgins"
"The Mustard Tree"
"Tares"
"Bad Fish"
"The Leaven"
"The Hid Treasure"
(Israel)
Kingdom
Announced
Matt. 3:1-6
The
Millennial
Kingdom
Renovation
Of The
Earth
By Fire
The
Perfect
Kingdom
Kingdom
Of Heaven
Merges Into
Kingdom
Of God
God All And In All
Eternity
From Creation To John The Baptist
Eternity
Kingdom Of God
Designed And Drawn
By Clarence Larkin
Fox Chase, Phila., Pa
CL 11/7/19
Copyrighted

I. WHAT THE CHURCH IS

1. The Church is a MYSTERY.

To the Old Testament Prophets the Kingdom was no "Mystery," neither was the fact that the Gentiles were to be saved. Rom. 9:25-26 (Hosea 2:23). The "Mystery" was what was to come in between the **"SUFFERINGS"** (Isa. 53:1-12) and the **"GLORY"** of Christ (Psa. 72:1-20. Dan. 7:13-14), that is, between the **"CROSS"** and the **"CROWN."** I Pet. 1:7-11. This "Mystery" was revealed to the Apostle Paul. Eph. 3:1-11. It was that God was going to form an entirely **"NEW THING,"** composed of both **Jew** and **Gentile**, to be called the Church. The purpose then of this Dispensation is not the bringing in of the "Kingdom," or the conversion of the world, but the **"out gathering"** of an **"Elect Body."—THE CHURCH.** Acts 15:14-18.

2. The Church is a BODY.

The Church is not only an "Elect Body," it is the **"BODY OF CHRIST."** Eph. 1:22-23. As its **"HEAD,"** there could be no Church until Christ had been raised from the dead and seated at the Right Hand of God, for God does not make **headless bodies.** In I Cor. 12:12-13 we are told how this "Body" is formed. It is formed by **"Spirit Baptism."** The Church then could not have existed until the **"Gift"** of the Holy Spirit on the "Day of Pentecost." Therefore the Church is composed only of those who are baptized into it by the Holy Spirit, that is by the "New Birth," and when the Holy Spirit ceases His work of "Baptism" the formation of the Church as Christ's **"BODY"** will cease, and the Church will be complete, and be taken out of the world. The Church then is not an **"Organization,"** but an **"ORGANISM"**—a **LIVING BODY.**

3. The Church is a BUILDING.

In I Cor. 3:9 the Church is spoken of as **"God's BUILDING,"** and in verse 16 as the **"TEMPLE OF GOD."** In Eph. 2:20-22, as a building in process of construction, it is spoken of as being **"fitly framed together"** and **growing into a "HOLY TEMPLE"** for the **"HABITATION OF GOD"** in the Person of the **HOLY SPIRIT.** As God's Presence was manifested in the Tabernacle by the **"Shekinah Glory,"** so now in this Dispensation, when Israel, nationally, is out of fellowship with God, and there is no Temple at Jerusalem, the Church is the **"Habitation of God"** on earth, where He manifests Himself through the "Third Person" of the Godhead—the **HOLY SPIRIT.** Matt. 18:20; 28:20. The "Spiritual Temple" of the Church could not be erected until Christ became the **"ROCK."** Matt. 16:18. I Cor. 3:9-11. Then upon Christ the "Rock," the "Foundation of the Apostles and New Testament Prophets" was laid (Eph. 2:20-22), and the first layer of the superstructure of 3000 "Living Stones" (I Pet. 2:5) was laid on the "Day of Pentecost" (Acts 2:41), and a few days later the second layer of 5000 was added (Acts 4:4), and so on, down the centuries, the Church has been growing as a **"HOLY TEMPLE."**

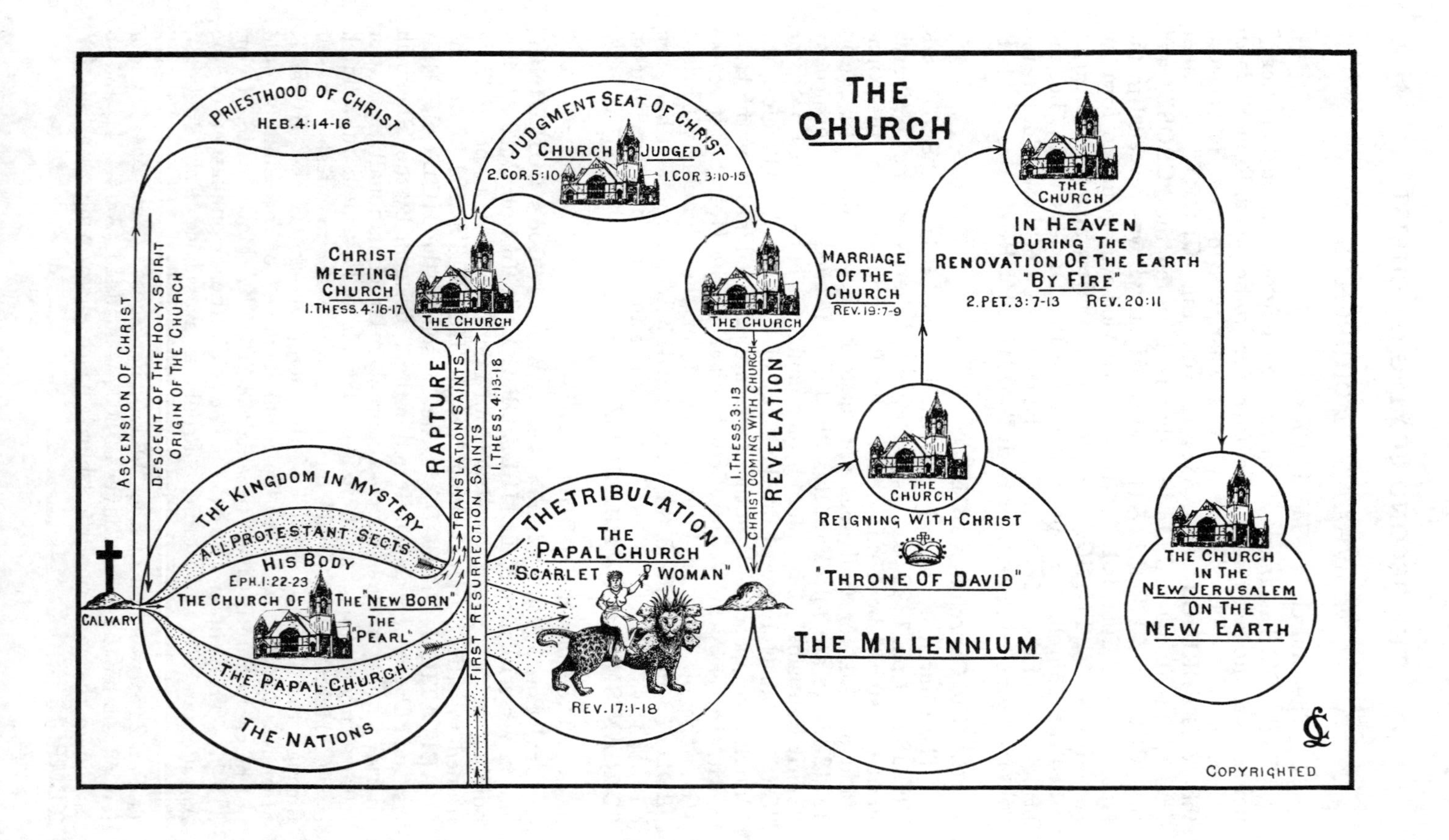
THE CHURCH
PRIESTHOOD OF CHRIST
HEB. 4:14-16
JUDGMENT SEAT OF CHRIST
CHURCH JUDGED
2. COR. 5:10
1. COR. 3:10-15
CHRIST MEETING CHURCH
1. THESS. 4:16-17
THE CHURCH
THE CHURCH
MARRIAGE OF THE CHURCH
REV. 19:7-9
THE CHURCH
IN HEAVEN
DURING THE
RENOVATION OF THE EARTH
"BY FIRE"
2. PET. 3:7-13
REV. 20:11
ASCENSION OF CHRIST
DESCENT OF THE HOLY SPIRIT
ORIGIN OF THE CHURCH
RAPTURE
TRANSLATION SAINTS
FIRST RESURRECTION SAINTS
1. THESS. 4:13-18
1. THESS. 3:13
CHRIST COMING WITH CHURCH
REVELATION
THE KINGDOM IN MYSTERY
ALL PROTESTANT SECTS
HIS BODY
EPH. 1:22-23
THE CHURCH OF THE "NEW BORN"
THE "PEARL"
THE PAPAL CHURCH
THE NATIONS
CALVARY
THE TRIBULATION
THE PAPAL CHURCH
"SCARLET WOMAN"
REV. 17:1-18
THE CHURCH
REIGNING WITH CHRIST
"THRONE OF DAVID"
THE MILLENNIUM
THE CHURCH
IN THE
NEW JERUSALEM
ON THE
NEW EARTH
CL
COPYRIGHTED

4. **The Church is to be the BRIDE OF CHRIST.**

At present the Church is a **"VIRGIN,"** but a Virgin **espoused.** II Cor. 11:2. The first Adam had his bride and so must the "Last Adam." Some hold that the Church cannot be both the **"Body"** and **"Bride"** of Christ, and that the "Bride" must be Israel. But we must not forget that there are **"Two Brides"** mentioned in the Scriptures, one in the Old Testament and the other in the New. The one in the Old Testament is "Israel," the Bride of Jehovah, the one in the New Testament is the "Church," the Bride of Christ. Because of her whoredoms Israel is at the present time a **"cast off WIFE."** When she ceases from her adulteries she will be taken back. Jer. 3:1-18; Ezek. 16:1-63; Hosea 2:1-23, 3:1-5. She will not be taken back as a "Virgin," but as a **"Wife."** But it is a **"VIRGIN"** that the Lamb (Christ) is to marry. So the "Wife" of the Old Testament cannot be the "Bride" (Virgin) of the New Testament. Again, the "Wife" (Israel) is to reside in the earthly Jerusalem during the Millennium, while the "Bride" (the Church) will reside in the New Jerusalem. These distinctions make it clear that Israel cannot be the "Bride" of Christ. Where the word "Wife" is used in Rev. 19:7-9; 21:9-10, it signifies the relation of the Bride to Christ **after** marriage, when she is no longer "Bride" but "Wife." As to the Church being both the "Body" and "Bride" of Christ, we have the type of Eve, who was **of the body of Adam** before she became his bride.

II. THE MISSION OF THE CHURCH

As we have seen, the Church is not an "Organization," but an **"Organism."** Therefore it is not a **"Social Club"** organized and supported for the benefit of its members. Neither is it a **"Place of Amusement"** to pander to the carnal nature of man. Nor is it a **"House of Merchandise"** for the sale of "Indulgences," or other commodities, whereby the money of the ungodly can be secured to save the penurious church member a little self sacrifice. Neither is it a **"Reform Bureau"** to save the **"bodies"** of men. The reformation of men is very commendable, as are all forms of "Social Service," but that is not the work of the Church. All the great philanthropic and civilizing agencies of the world are **"By-Products"** of Christianity, but the "Mission" of the Church is her **"COMMISSION"** to **"Evangelize"** the world. Mark 16:15-16. Acts 1:7-8. The **"Kingdom Idea"** has robbed the Church of her **"UPWARD LOOK,"** and of the **"BLESSED HOPE."** There cannot be any **"Imminent Coming"** to those who are seeking to **"Set up the Kingdom."** The "Kingdom Idea" has robbed the Church of the "Pilgrim" and "Martyr Spirit," and caused it to go down into Egypt for help. When the Church enters into an **"Alliance with the World,"** and seeks the help of Parliaments, Congresses, Legislatures, Federations and Reform Societies, largely made up of ungodly men and women, she loses her **"SPIRITUAL POWER"** and becomes helpless as a redeeming force. The end of such an "Alliance" will be a "Religious Political Regime" that will pave the way for the revelation of Satan's great **"Religious Political Leader"** and **"Superman"**—the **ANTICHRIST.**

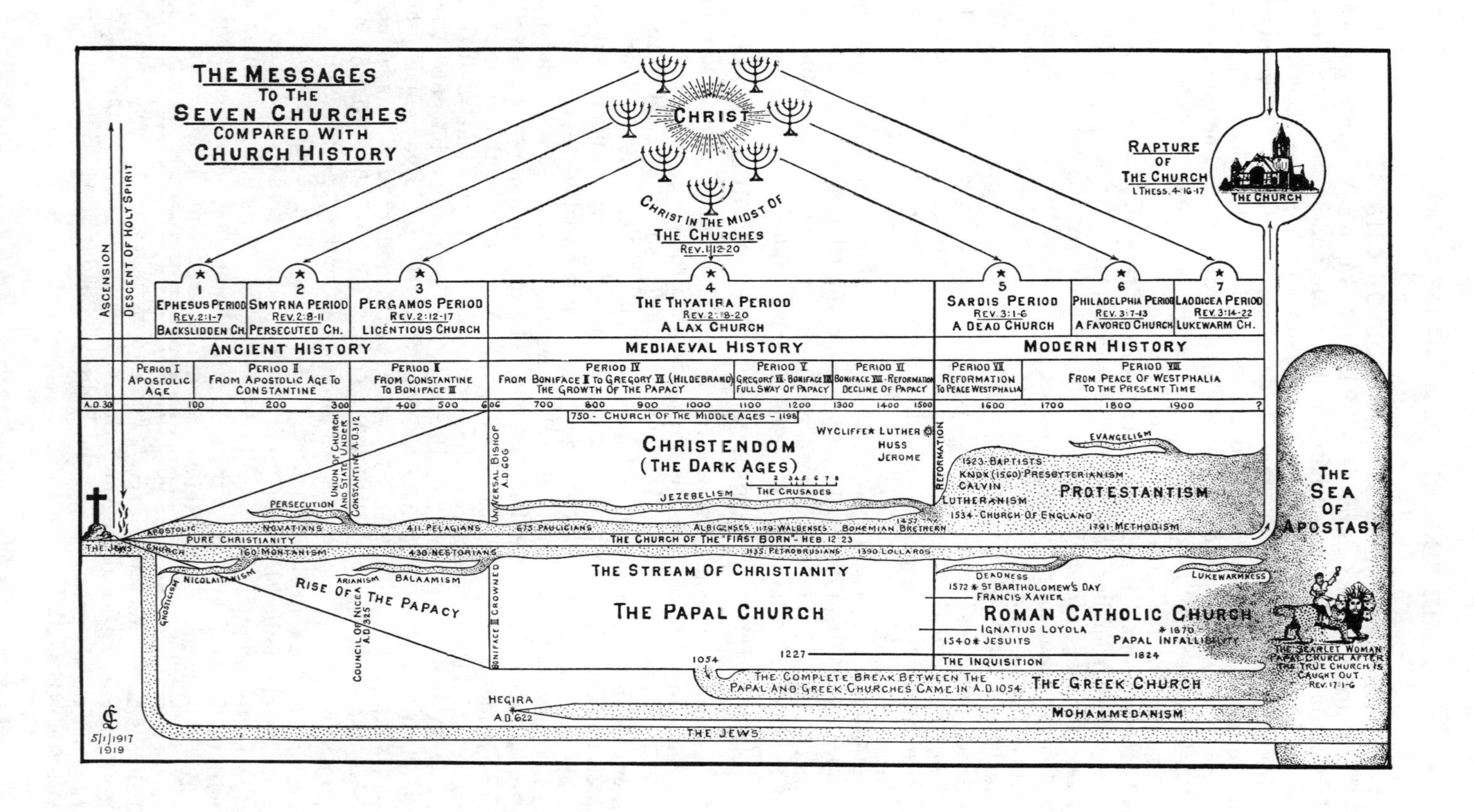

THE MESSAGES
TO THE
SEVEN CHURCHES
COMPARED WITH
CHURCH HISTORY
CHRIST
CHRIST IN THE MIDST OF
THE CHURCHES
REV. 1:12-20
RAPTURE
OF
THE CHURCH
I. THESS. 4-16-17
THE CHURCH
ASCENSION
DESCENT OF HOLY SPIRIT
1 EPHESUS PERIOD REV. 2:1-7 BACKSLIDDEN CH.
2 SMYRNA PERIOD REV. 2:8-11 PERSECUTED CH.
3 PERGAMOS PERIOD REV. 2:12-17 LICENTIOUS CHURCH
4 THE THYATIRA PERIOD REV. 2:18-20 A LAX CHURCH
5 SARDIS PERIOD REV. 3:1-6 A DEAD CHURCH
6 PHILADELPHIA PERIOD REV. 3:7-13 A FAVORED CHURCH
7 LAODICEA PERIOD REV. 3:14-22 LUKEWARM CH.
ANCIENT HISTORY
MEDIAEVAL HISTORY
MODERN HISTORY
PERIOD I APOSTOLIC AGE
PERIOD II FROM APOSTOLIC AGE TO CONSTANTINE
PERIOD III FROM CONSTANTINE TO BONIFACE III
PERIOD IV FROM BONIFACE III TO GREGORY VII (HILDEBRAND) THE GROWTH OF THE PAPACY
PERIOD V GREGORY VII - BONIFACE VIII FULL SWAY OF PAPACY
PERIOD VI BONIFACE VIII - REFORMATION DECLINE OF PAPACY
PERIOD VII REFORMATION TO PEACE WESTPHALIA
PERIOD VIII FROM PEACE OF WESTPHALIA TO THE PRESENT TIME
A.D. 30 100 200 300 400 500 606 700 800 900 1000 1100 1200 1300 1400 1500 1600 1700 1800 1900 ?
750 - CHURCH OF THE MIDDLE AGES - 1198
CHRISTENDOM
(THE DARK AGES)
WYCLIFFE LUTHER
HUSS
JEROME
REFORMATION
UNION OF CHURCH AND STATE UNDER CONSTANTINE A.D. 312
UNIVERSAL BISHOP A.D. 606
PERSECUTION
JEZEBELISM
THE CRUSADES
EVANGELISM
1523 BAPTISTS
KNOX (1560) PRESBYTERIANISM
CALVIN
LUTHERANISM
PROTESTANTISM
1534 CHURCH OF ENGLAND
1791 METHODISM
APOSTOLIC
NOVATIANS
411 PELAGIANS
673 PAULICIANS
ALBIGENSES 1179 WALDENSES
1457 BOHEMIAN BRETHERN
THE JEWS
CHURCH
PURE CHRISTIANITY
THE CHURCH OF THE "FIRST BORN" - HEB. 12:23
160 MONTANISM
430 NESTORIANS
1135 PETROBRUSIANS
1390 LOLLARDS
THE SEA
OF
APOSTASY
THE STREAM OF CHRISTIANITY
THE PAPAL CHURCH
GNOSTICISM
NICOLAITANISM
ARIANISM
BALAAMISM
RISE OF THE PAPACY
COUNCIL OF NICEA A.D. 325
BONIFACE III CROWNED
DEADNESS
1572 ST BARTHOLOMEW'S DAY
FRANCIS XAVIER
LUKEWARMNESS
ROMAN CATHOLIC CHURCH
IGNATIUS LOYOLA
1540 JESUITS
1870
PAPAL INFALLIBILITY
1227
1824
THE INQUISITION
1054
THE COMPLETE BREAK BETWEEN THE
PAPAL AND GREEK CHURCHES CAME IN A.D. 1054.
THE GREEK CHURCH
THE SCARLET WOMAN
PAPAL CHURCH AFTER
THE TRUE CHURCH IS
CAUGHT OUT
REV. 17:1-6
HEGIRA
A.D. 622
MOHAMMEDANISM
THE JEWS
5/1/1917
1919

III. THE HISTORY OF THE CHURCH

It is the Divine way to give, at the beginning of some new thing which God is going to do in the earth, a "Prophetic Foreview" of its history. The "Prophetic Foreview" of Israel's history is given in Deuteronomy, chapters 27 to 30, and of the Gentiles in Daniel, chapters 2 and 7. Both of these down to date have been literally fulfilled. It follows therefore that we should find somewhere in the Scriptures a "Prophetic Foreview" of the History of the Christian Church. This History we find in the Book of Revelation, chapters 2 and 3, in the "Messages to the Seven Churches of Asia." These were typical churches and are descriptive of **"Seven Church Periods."** The Prophetic meaning of these "Messages" was hidden to the early Church because time was required for Church History to develop and be written so a comparison could be made to reveal the correspondence. For a full description of this correspondence see the author's work on the Book of Revelation. An outline is shown on the accompanying Chart. We are now living in the "Laodicean" or "Last Stage" of the Church's History in this Dispensation, which reveals the fact that the next "Event" is the "Return of the Lord," who will **"SPUE"** the **"Lukewarm"** Church out of His mouth. Rev. 3: 14-16.

IV. THE PRESENT LOCATION OF THE CHURCH IN THE SPIRITUAL HEAVENS

What is true of the "Physical Heavens" is true of the "Spiritual Heavens." In the last book of the Old Testament Jesus is called the **"Sun of Righteousness."** Mal. 4: 2. When He was on the earth He declared Himself to be the **"LIGHT OF THE WORLD"** (John 9: 5), but that **"LIGHT"** was eclipsed by Calvary. From this we see that earth's "Spiritual Day" or "Night" is dependent on whether Jesus as the "Sun of Righteousness" is visible or invisible, and is determined by His presence or absence. See the Chart, "Night and Day." Page 54. As Jesus is not now visibly present on the earth the period in which we are living is **NIGHT,** and we should expect only such illumination as the night can furnish, which in the physical heavens is the Moon and Stars, and on the earth artificial light. This is **"MAN'S DAY"** (I Cor. 4: 3 margin), a day of intellectual light, and as we have improved our artificial lights, and now use electricity where once we used candles, so men are boasting of the improvements they have made in intellectual lights, such as scientific discoveries and the various new religious cults, and have replaced "Divine Revelation" by the "Light of Reason," and reject the illumination of the Holy Spirit for the **"ignis fatuus"** of **"SEDUCING SPIRITS."** I Tim. 4: 1. II Pet. 2: 1-2.

If this is the **"Night"** of this Dispensation what luminary in the "Spiritual Firmament" are we to look to for light? What luminary gives light in the physical heavens at night? The Moon. Then we must look to the **"MOON"** of the "Spiritual Firmament" for light, and that is the Church. The Moon shines by reflected light from the Sun, so the Church shines by reflected light from the "Sun of Right-

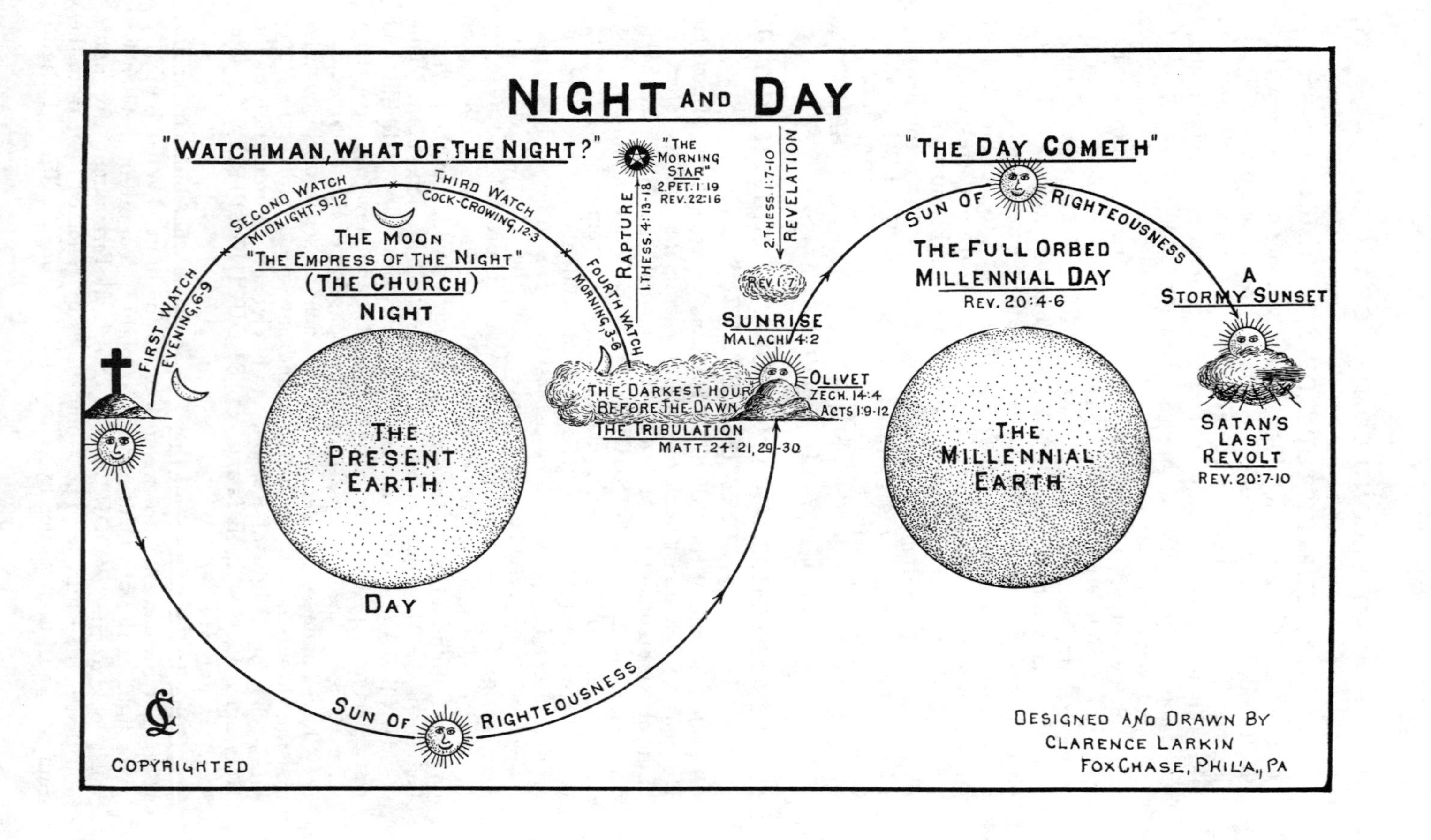
NIGHT AND DAY
"WATCHMAN, WHAT OF THE NIGHT?"
"THE DAY COMETH"
FIRST WATCH
EVENING, 6-9
SECOND WATCH
MIDNIGHT, 9-12
THIRD WATCH
COCK-CROWING, 12-3
FOURTH WATCH
MORNING, 3-6
THE MOON
"THE EMPRESS OF THE NIGHT"
(THE CHURCH)
NIGHT
THE PRESENT EARTH
DAY
SUN OF RIGHTEOUSNESS
RAPTURE
1. THESS. 4:13-18
"THE MORNING STAR"
2. PET. 1:19
REV. 22:16
2. THESS. 1:7-10
REVELATION
REV. 1:7
SUNRISE
MALACHI 4:2
OLIVET
ZECH. 14:4
ACTS 1:9-12
THE DARKEST HOUR BEFORE THE DAWN
THE TRIBULATION
MATT. 24:21, 29-30
SUN OF RIGHTEOUSNESS
THE FULL ORBED MILLENNIAL DAY
REV. 20:4-6
THE MILLENNIAL EARTH
A STORMY SUNSET
SATAN'S LAST REVOLT
REV. 20:7-10
CL
COPYRIGHTED
DESIGNED AND DRAWN BY
CLARENCE LARKIN
FOX CHASE, PHIL'A., PA

eousness." The Moon is only visible in the night, so the Church is only visible in the night of this Dispensation. When the "Sun of Righteousness" arises, and the **"Day of the Lord,"** or **"Millennial Day,"** dawns, the Church will become invisible, not because she will cease to exist, but because her light will pale before the greater light of the "Sun of Righteousness."

What time is it then on the Dial of God's Timepiece? It is **NIGHT.** But what time of the Night? Let the Apostle Paul answer. "The night is **far spent,** the day **IS AT HAND."** Rom. 13:12. Jesus divided the night into **"Four Watches."**

> "Watch ye therefore: for ye know not when the 'Master of the House' **cometh,** at **EVEN,** or at **MIDNIGHT,** or at the **COCK-CROWING,** or in the **MORNING."** Mark 13:35.

The "Four Watches" are—

FIRST WATCH:—"Evening." From 6-9 P. M. Corresponding to "Apostolic Times."

SECOND WATCH:—"Midnight." From 9-12 P. M. Corresponding to the "Dark Ages."

THIRD WATCH:—"Cock-crowing." From 12-3 A. M. Corresponding to the "Period of the Reformation."

FOURTH WATCH:—"Morning." From 3-6 A. M. We are living in the **"MORNING WATCH."**

How beautifully this is pictured prophetically in the experience of the Disciples on that night on the Sea of Galilee when the winds were **contrary.** Matt. 14:22-33. After the miracle of feeding the 5000 Jesus constrained His Disciples to embark in their boat for the Galilean side of the Lake while He sent the multitude away, and then went into a mountain apart to pray. When the Disciples were half-way across the Sea they were caught in one of those sudden and severe storms that sweep over the Sea of Galilee, and, because the winds were **"contrary,"** they **"toiled in rowing,"** and could make no progress. Then it was that Jesus came to their rescue walking on the sea, that became a liquid floor, smooth and level, beneath His Holy Feet. The Disciples did not dare to turn back, for that would have been to fail in duty, but Jesus saw their faithfulness and was on His way to their rescue. They did not know it, but Jesus was **COMING,** and we are told the time, that it was the **"FOURTH WATCH"** of the night—the **"MORNING WATCH."**

That tempest tossed boat on the Sea of Galilee is a type of the Christian Church breasting the waves of sin and worldliness and false doctrine of this Dispensation. It is long past midnight, and it seems as if all the available forces of evil are associating themselves together, to, by one cyclonic effort, swamp the frail bark of the Church, and cause it to be engulfed in the waves of sin and unbelief. Over against it blow the **"CONTRARY WINDS"** of **Atheism, Scepticism, Infidelity, Ritualism, Formalism, Unitarianism, Rationalism, Spiritualism** and the **"False Cults."** To many it is a dark hour. **Sabbath Desecra-**

tion, Lukewarmness, Indifference, and **Worldliness** are sapping the strength of the toilers in the boat. The clouds thicken and blacken, and the sky becomes more overcast as the **"Falling Away"** advances. II Thess. 2:3. Many are pessimistic. But amid the deepening gloom we must not forget that the "darkest hour" of the night in just before the dawn. Jesus has not forgotten His Disciples. He sees them **"toiling in rowing."** Soon He will leave the "Place of Intercession" and come to their rescue. Soon above the clouds that are now beginning to hide the "Empress of the Night"—the Church, as she sinks toward the horizon, will be seen—

"THE MORNING STAR."

The "Morning Star" is the herald of the coming day. It is seen only by the **"Watchers"** or the early risers. In the "Spiritual Heavens" Christ is also the **"BRIGHT AND MORNING STAR."** Rev. 22:16. II Pet. 1:19. He is the **"Morning Star"** when He comes and takes out His Church at the "Rapture," He is the **"Sun of Righteousness"** when He comes back **with His Church** at the "Revelation" to reign on the earth. The appearance of the "Morning Star" only intensifies the darkness of the night. So between the appearing of Christ as the "Morning Star," and His coming as the "Sun of Righteousness," there will be a period of great darkness, known as "The Great Tribulation." Matt. 24:21, 29-31. We are living in the "Fourth Watch," soon the "Morning Star" will appear, and the Church will be "Caught Out." Then will follow the "Great Tribulation," and after it will come the **"SUNRISE"** of that bright "Millennial Day," when Christ, as the **"SUN OF RIGHTEOUSNESS,"** shall shine in full orbed splendor in the "Spiritual Heavens" of a **"DAY"** that is to be 1000 years long.

The Drag Net. Matt. 13:47-50.

Is the World to be Converted Before Christ Comes

The common opinion is, that the Gospel is to be preached in all the world until the whole world is converted, then will follow the Millennium, after which Christ will come back and there will be a "General Resurrection" and a "General Judgment," and the earth will be destroyed by fire, time will cease and eternity begin. Is this the "Program" of the Scriptures?

After nearly 1900 years of Gospel preaching are the churches of Christ throughout the world multiplying with great rapidity? Are the congregations in the churches increasing in numbers and taxing the seating capacity of the churches to accommodate them? Are the churches in downtown and congested districts stronger and more crowded and influential than ever? Are the professing followers of Christ more consecrated, spiritual, and benevolent than ever before? Are Christian men and women taking their religion into their business and social affairs as never before? Are our young men and women forsaking the world in large numbers and giving themselves to the ministry and missionary work? Are the treasuries of the missionary societies burdened with an oversupply of funds? Have our churches no difficulty in meeting their financial needs? Have the cities, towns and countries of the world, where the Gospel has been preached for centuries, become thoroughly Christianized, so that today worldliness and sin is largely unknown in them? Is it a fact that the children of Christian parents naturally and willingly accept the Gospel so that Christianity is growing as rapidly as the birthrate in Christian families? Is Christianity so influencing business, commercial and manufacturing enterprises, that business is now being conducted on Christian principles? Are the combinations of capital and labor run on the basis of the "Golden Rule," and in the "Spirit of Christ"? Are the nations of the earth beating their swords into plowshares, and their spears into pruning hooks? Are they dismantling their navies and diminishing the size of their armies? Have cities and towns ceased building jails, prisons, penitentiaries and houses of correction? Is there no further use for officers of the law and courts of Justice? Is the government of our towns and cities and nations more free from misrule than ever before? Is the law more honored, and are there fewer divorces and more purity of life in the 20th century than in the 19th?

To ask these questions is to answer them. Is the Gospel then a failure, or have we misinterpreted its mission? There are three lines of argument we may follow in seeking our answer.

I. **The "HISTORICAL" Argument.**

The history of the world, as outlined in the Scriptures, has consisted up to the present Dispensation, of five Dispensations, all marked as the Rev. A. T. Pierson, D.D., so clearly outlined, by seven features essentially the same—"First, an advance in fullness and

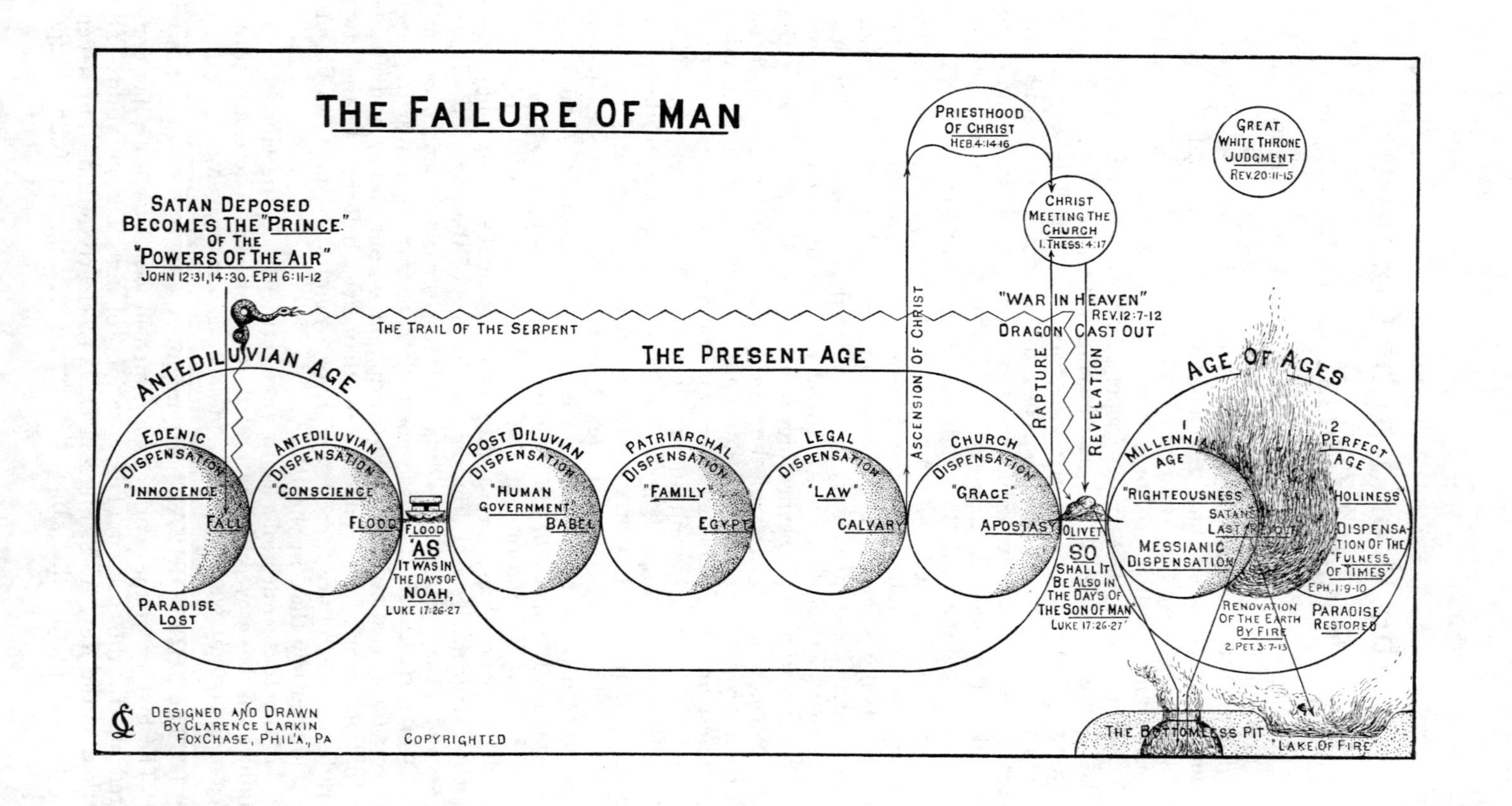
THE FAILURE OF MAN
SATAN DEPOSED BECOMES THE "PRINCE" OF THE "POWERS OF THE AIR"
JOHN 12:31, 14:30. EPH 6:11-12
THE TRAIL OF THE SERPENT
PRIESTHOOD OF CHRIST
HEB 4:14-16
CHRIST MEETING THE CHURCH
I. THESS. 4:17
GREAT WHITE THRONE JUDGMENT
REV. 20:11-15
"WAR IN HEAVEN"
REV. 12:7-12
DRAGON CAST OUT
ASCENSION OF CHRIST
RAPTURE
REVELATION
ANTEDILUVIAN AGE
EDENIC DISPENSATION
"INNOCENCE"
FALL
PARADISE LOST
ANTEDILUVIAN DISPENSATION
"CONSCIENCE"
FLOOD
FLOOD
'AS IT WAS IN THE DAYS OF NOAH,
LUKE 17:26-27
THE PRESENT AGE
POST DILUVIAN DISPENSATION
"HUMAN GOVERNMENT"
BABEL
PATRIARCHAL DISPENSATION
"FAMILY"
EGYPT
LEGAL DISPENSATION
'LAW'
CALVARY
CHURCH DISPENSATION
"GRACE"
APOSTASY
OLIVET
SO SHALL IT BE ALSO IN THE DAYS OF THE SON OF MAN'
LUKE 17:26-27
AGE OF AGES
1 MILLENNIAL AGE
"RIGHTEOUSNESS"
SATAN'S LAST REVOLT
MESSIANIC DISPENSATION
2 PERFECT AGE
"HOLINESS"
DISPENSATION OF THE "FULNESS OF TIMES"
EPH. 1:9-10
RENOVATION OF THE EARTH BY FIRE
2. PET. 3:7-13
PARADISE RESTORED
THE BOTTOMLESS PIT
"LAKE OF FIRE"
DESIGNED AND DRAWN BY CLARENCE LARKIN FOXCHASE, PHIL'A., PA
COPYRIGHTED

clearness of revelation; then gradual spiritual declension; then conformity to the world ending with amalgamation with the world; then a gigantic civilization brilliant but Godless; then parallel development of evil and good; then an **Apostasy,** and finally a **Catastrophe.**" These five Dispensations were—(1) The Edenic, that of "**Innocence.**" It ended in the "**FALL OF MAN.**" (2) The Ante-Diluvian, that of "**Conscience.**" It ended in the "**FLOOD.**" (3) The Post-Diluvian, that of "**Human Government.**" It ended in the "**Confusion of Tongues**" at "**Babel.**" (4) The Patriarchal, that of the "**Family.**" It ended in slavery for Israel in **EGYPT.** (5) The Legal, that of "**Law.**" It ended in the "**CRUCIFIXION OF CHRIST**" and the scattering over the world of the Jewish people. See the Chart, "The Failure of Man," page 58. Now how is this Dispensation of "**Grace**" in which we are living to end? Is it to end differently from those that preceded it? For our answer we must turn from History to Prophecy.

II. **The "BIBLICAL" Argument.**

For the sake of brevity and to avoid repetition we will limit our argument to the words of Christ Himself. For further proof read the Chapter on "The Signs of the Times," page 65. In Matt. 13:1-52 we have a "Parabolic" prophetic description of the character of this Dispensation. In the Parable of "**The Sower**" we find that only ¼ of the seed sown got in, grew up, and brought forth fruit, and of that ¼ only a small part brought forth a 100 fold. In the Parable of the "**Wheat and Tares**" we find that the Wheat and the Tares are to grow **side by side** until the Harvest, which is the end of this Dispensation, and that they will ripen into fullness, each **after his own kind,** until the angel reapers shall gather out the Tares, preparatory to burning them after the Wheat has been safely gathered into the "Heavenly Barn." In the Parable of the "**Mustard Tree**" we see how the visible church is sought as a "roosting place" by the "birds of the air," the emissaries of Satan (Matt. 13:4, 19), who lodge in its branches, not so much for shelter as to befoul the tree. These are the "False Teachers" of II Pet. 2:1-2, which are so evident in our day. In the Parable of the "**Leaven**" we see the spread of "Evil Doctrine" in the sphere of the Christian Church. Leaven in the Scriptures is a type of evil. It cannot be a type of the Gospel, for the Gospel does not spread of itself, while Leaven does. And as the Leaven is to permeate and contaminate the whole mass of meal, it is clear that "Evil Doctrine" will prevail in the Church in the closing days of this Dispensation. Passing over the 5th and 6th Parables that refer to Israel, the "Hid Treasure," and the Church, the "Pearl," we come to the Parable of the "**Dragnet.**" From this Parable we see that at the close of this Dispensation, instead of the whole "**sea of humanity**" being in the Gospel net, only a small proportion will be caught, and of them not all **are good,** for the good fish are gathered into vessels, and the bad are cast away." From these Parables we see that the world is not to be converted before Christ returns. For a full explanation of these Parables see my book on "Dispensational Truth."

In His "Olivet Discourse" (Matt. 24:1-31), delivered by Jesus on the Tuesday night before His Crucifixion, in answer to the Disciples' question—"And what shall be the **'SIGN'** of Thy Coming, and of the end of the **world** (Age)"—Jesus said—

> "Ye shall hear of **wars** and **rumors of wars** . . . nation shall rise against nation, and kingdom against kingdom: and there shall be **famines,** and **pestilences,** and **earthquakes,** in divers places. All these are the **BEGINNING OF SORROWS.** . . . Many 'False Prophets' shall rise, and shall **deceive** many. And because **iniquity shall abound,** the love of many shall **WAX COLD.** . . . Then shall be great **'Tribulation,'** such as was not since the beginning of the world . . . and except those days **should be shortened,** there should be no flesh **SAVED:** but for the elect's (Jews) sake those days **shall be shortened."**

That Jesus did not here refer to the "Tribulation" that befell the Jews at the destruction of Jerusalem in A. D. 70 is clear, for He adds— **"IMMEDIATELY** after the **'Tribulation of those days** shall the **sun be darkened,** and the **moon shall not give her light,** and the **stars shall fall from heaven,** and the **powers** (Evil Powers) **of the heavens shall be shaken.** (None of these things happened at the Destruction of Jerusalem): and **THEN** shall appear the **'SIGN** (a cloud) **OF THE SON OF MAN'** in heaven (the atmospheric heavens): and **THEN** shall all the 'Tribes of the Earth' **MOURN,** and they shall see the 'Son of Man' coming in the **clouds of heaven** with **POWER** and **GREAT GLORY."**

These words reveal the fact that when Jesus comes back, it will be **IMMEDIATELY** after a period of wars, famines, pestilences, earthquakes and a season of "Great Tribulation," that if it is not shortened will destroy **all flesh,** and that when He comes back, instead of being received joyfully, the "Tribes of the Earth" shall **MOURN,** men's hearts failing for **FEAR** (Luke 21:25-27), all Kindreds (nations) of the earth shall **WAIL** because of Him (Rev. 1:7), and the **kings** of the earth, and the **great men,** and the **rich men,** and the **chief captains,** and the **mighty men,** and every **bondman** and every **free man,** shall hide themselves in the dens and in the rocks of the mountains; and say to the mountains and rocks—**"FALL ON US, AND HIDE US FROM THE FACE OF HIM THAT SITTETH ON THE THRONE, AND FROM THE "WRATH OF THE LAMB:" FOR THE GREAT DAY OF HIS WRATH IS COME; AND WHO SHALL BE ABLE TO STAND?** Rev. 6:15-17.

What an awful time is here revealed. It is not a picture of a Gospel converted world gladly welcoming the return of its Lord, but of a panic stricken world seeking to escape from His presence, when He shall be revealed in **"FLAMING FIRE"** taking **VENGEANCE** on them that **know not God** (the Heathen), and that **obey not the "Gospel of Christ"** (the Wicked). II Thess. 1:7-10. Truly Christ will not find **"THE FAITH,"** covering the earth, when He returns. Luke 18:8.

III. **The "WORLD" Argument.**

One of the objections to the Pre-Millennial Return of Christ is that it cannot be squared with the belief in the **"Continuance of History."** But it will no more interfere with the "Continuance of History" than the First Coming of Christ did. The world moved on then just as it did before, and so it will after His Second Coming. The "Second Coming" will be but an **"episode"** or **"event"** in history. Another objection is, that it is not **scientific.** That it nullifies the **"Evolutionary Development"** of Christianity, and is a confession that the **"Spiritual Forces"** of God are unable to save the world, and that God will have to resort to **"Miraculous Militarism,"** and send the **"Armies of Heaven,"** under the leadership of Christ, to save Himself from defeat. Rev. 19:11-21.

All that is needed to answer these objections is to compare the boasted civilization of today with that of 100 years ago, to see that the civilization of today has degenerated. The nations today are like **"wild beasts"** preying upon each other, as foretold by Daniel. Dan. 7:1-28. The boasted genius of today is engaged not so much in constructive work, as in the invention of destructive instruments of war. Men and women and nations have become brutalized, and appear to be but **"veneered barbarians."** The **"Blood Poison"** of **SIN,** no longer hidden in some internal organ of the "Body Politic," is now revealed on the surface, and is seen in the lawlessness of the world. As just before the Flood, the earth is filled with **"corruption"** and **"violence"** (Gen. 6:11-12), as Jesus said it would be, when He said—

> "**AS** it was in the **'Days of Noah,' SO** shall it be **ALSO** in the **'Days of the Son of Man.'** " Luke 17:26.

A comparison of those "Noah Days" with the present will indicate that we are living in the last days of this Dispensation.

NOAH DAYS

The prominent characteristics of the days shortly before the Flood were—

1. A tendency to worship God simply as a **"Creator,"** and not as **"JEHOVAH,"** requiring **Atonement for sin.** For illustration the offerings of Cain and Abel. Gen. 4:3-8. So today men make light of a **"BLOOD Atonement."**

2. A rapid advance in **Civilization** and in the **"Arts"** and **"Sciences"** that led to ease and luxury. Gen. 4:19-22. This is true of today when we consider all the modern inventions that tend to comfort and travel and the transmission of news.

3. There was a union of the **"Holy Line"** of Seth and the **"Wicked Line"** of Cain, so that at the time of the Flood there were only 8 persons fit to be saved in the Ark. Gen. 7:7, 13. So today there is an "Unholy Alliance" between the Church and the World.

4. A vast increase and **"Congestion of Population"** in the cities. Gen. 4:16-17; 6:1. This tended to all kinds of wickedness and corruption. Gen. 6:5, 11-12. This is true of our great cities today, they are **hotbeds of crime.**

5. Undue **"Prominence"** of the "Female Sex." God's sentence upon Eve was that she should be subject to her husband (Gen. 3:16), but the record of the cause of the Flood reveals the fact that the women of those days were not "stay at homes," but were prominent in public affairs. How true is this of today.

6. **"Unlawful Intercourse"** of the **"Denizens of the Air"** (Angels in human form) with the **"Daughters of Men."** Gen. 6:2-4. For a full explanation of this see my book on "The Spirit World." The revival of Spiritualism and the resorting to **"Familiar"** or **"SEDUCING SPIRITS"** is one of the "Signs" of the **"Latter Times,"** or last days of this Dispensation. I Tim. 4:1-3. The restored city of Babylon will be the **"hold"** of all kind of **"FOUL SPIRITS."** Rev. 18:2.

7. The **"Rejection"** of the Preaching of Enoch and Noah. Jude 14-15. Today the preaching of the Pre-Millennial Coming of the Lord is scoffed at (II Pet. 3:3-4) and turned away from, and teachers who will **"itch the ear"** with some smooth doctrine are popular. I Tim. 4:3-4.

From these seven marked features of the "Days of Noah" we see, by comparison, that we are bordering on the "Days of the Son of Man."

What we witness today is not a world converted by the preaching of the Gospel, but a **"Godless Civilization"** that has been built up by Satan in his attempt to bring in a **"MOCK MILLENNIUM."** As a world converting power, after nearly 1900 years of effort, the Gospel has been a failure. A careful examination of the "History of Missions" reveals the fact that the world today is farther away from being converted than it was at the close of the First Century. Modern missions began with William Carey in A. D. 1792. The population of the world in A. D. 1792 was estimated to be 731,000,000, as follows:

Heathen	420,000,000
Mohammedans	130,000,000
Roman Catholics	100,000,000
Protestants	44,000,000
Greek Church	30,000,000
Jews	7,000,000
	731,000,000

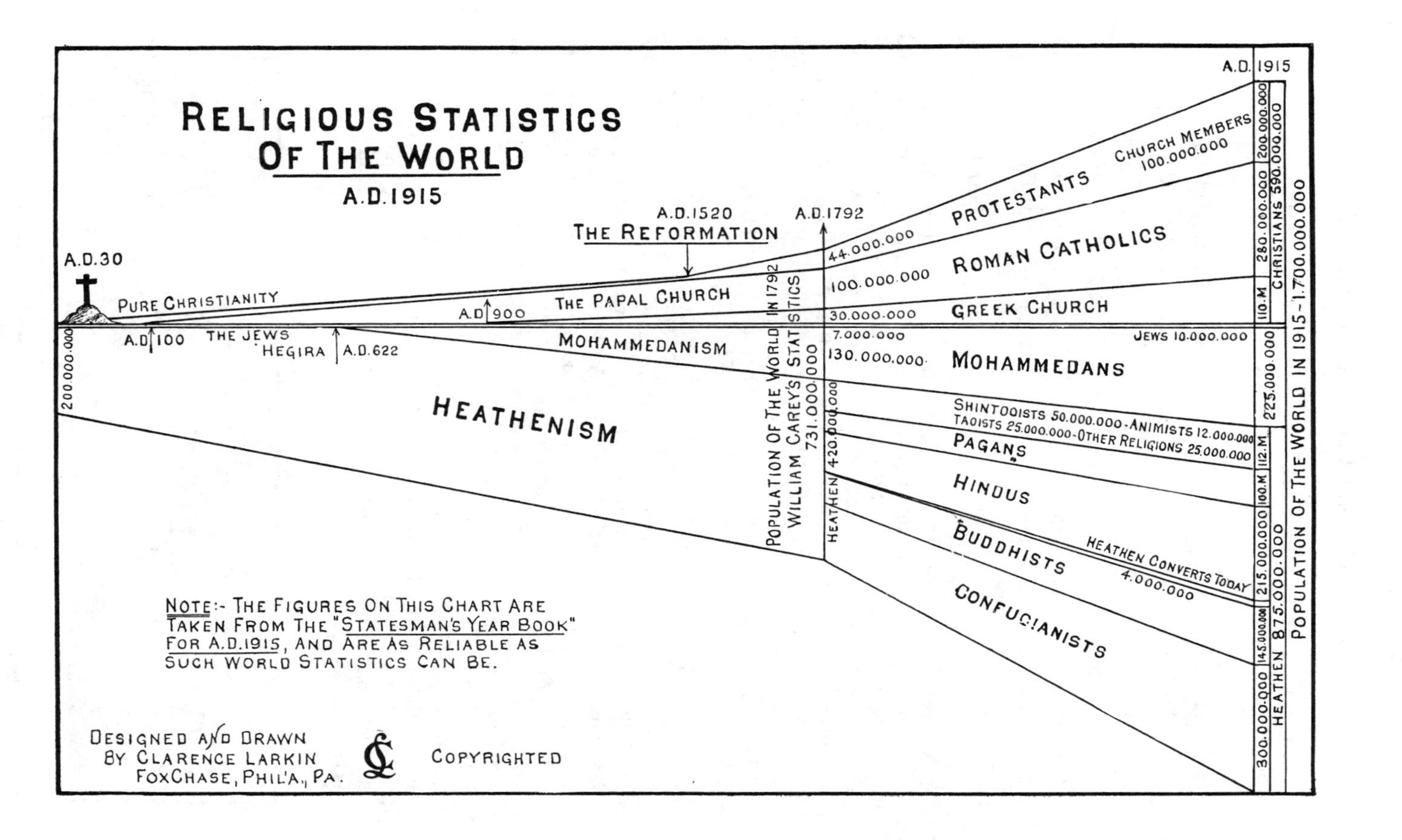
RELIGIOUS STATISTICS
OF THE WORLD
A.D. 1915
A.D. 30
PURE CHRISTIANITY
A.D. 100
THE JEWS
HEGIRA
A.D. 622
A.D. 900
THE PAPAL CHURCH
A.D. 1520
THE REFORMATION
MOHAMMEDANISM
HEATHENISM
200.000.000
A.D. 1792
POPULATION OF THE WORLD IN 1792
WILLIAM CAREY'S STATISTICS
731.000.000
HEATHEN 420.000.000
44.000.000
100.000.000
30.000.000
7.000.000
130.000.000
PROTESTANTS
CHURCH MEMBERS 100.000.000
ROMAN CATHOLICS
GREEK CHURCH
JEWS 10.000.000
MOHAMMEDANS
SHINTOOISTS 50.000.000 - ANIMISTS 12.000.000
TAOISTS 25.000.000 - OTHER RELIGIONS 25.000.000
PAGANS
HINDUS
BUDDHISTS
HEATHEN CONVERTS TODAY 4.000.000
CONFUCIANISTS
A.D. 1915
200.000.000
280.000.000
110.M
CHRISTIANS 590.000.000
225.000.000
112.M
100.M
215.000.000
145.000.000
300.000.000
HEATHEN 875.000.000
POPULATION OF THE WORLD IN 1915 - 1.700.000.000
NOTE:- THE FIGURES ON THIS CHART ARE TAKEN FROM THE "STATESMAN'S YEAR BOOK" FOR A.D. 1915, AND ARE AS RELIABLE AS SUCH WORLD STATISTICS CAN BE.
DESIGNED AND DRAWN
BY CLARENCE LARKIN
FOXCHASE, PHIL'A., PA.
COPYRIGHTED

The population of the world, from reliable statistics, see the Chart "Religious Statistics," page 63, was, in A. D. 1915, 1,700,000,000, as follows:

Heathen	875,000,000
Mohammedans	225,000,000
Roman Catholics	280,000,000
Protestants	200,000,000
Greek Church	110,000,000
Jews	10,000,000
	1,700,000,000

After 123 years of Foreign Missionary work, from A. D. 1792 to A. D. 1915, there are today in round numbers only about 4,000,000 professing Christians in Heathen lands, which include China, India and Africa. Counting the Roman Catholics, the Greek Church, and the Protestants, only one-third of the world's population is nominally Christian, and of the Protestants only one-half, or 100,000,000, are church members, and of them possibly 50 per cent have never been born again. If in 123 years, from A. D. 1792 to A. D. 1915, Heathenism has increased from 420,000,000 to 875,000,000, and converts from Heathenism have only increased in the same time from the first convert to 4,000,000, is it not evident that there are more than a 100 times as many persons born into the world each year than are **"NEW BORN?"** How many centuries at this rate will it take the world **not to be converted,** but to **BECOME HEATHEN?** Then we must not forget that, alarmed at the spread of Christianity, there is a revival of the Heathen religions, and that the sending out of "Modern Theology" missionaries is hampering our Foreign Missionary Work. What do these facts and figures prove? Do they prove that the Gospel is a failure? No! The Gospel has never failed, and never will fail. It is the **"Power of God"** unto **SALVATION.** Rom. 1:16. The "Gospel" is accomplishing just the mission that God intended it to. What these figures prove is, that it is not God's purpose to convert the world in this Dispensation, but simply to gather out an **"Elect Body"—THE CHURCH.**

The Signs of the Times

While we cannot name the exact date of the Lord's Return its nearness may be known by the **character** of the Times. As to this the New Testament gives no uncertain sound. In Dan. 12:4, 9-10, we read, "But thou, O Daniel, shut up the words, and seal the Book, even to the **'TIME OF THE END'**: many shall run to and fro, and knowledge shall be increased. . . . Go thy way, Daniel: for the words are closed up and sealed till the **'TIME OF THE END.'** Many shall be purified, and made white, and tried; but the wicked shall do wickedly: and none of the wicked shall understand; but the **WISE SHALL UNDERSTAND."** These words declare that the prophecies of Daniel were to be **"shut up"** and **"sealed"** until the **"TIME OF THE END."** This expression does not mean the **"end of Time,"** but is the angelic messenger's way of referring to the "Last Days" of the "Times of the Gentiles." At which time he declares that the Book will be **"unsealed,"** and **"knowledge shall be increased."** What is here meant is **"prophetic knowledge"** of the things recorded in the Book of Daniel and other prophetic writings of the Scriptures.. This is made clear by the statement that only the **"wise"** shall understand. That is, those who are enlightened by the Holy Spirit, and not those who merely have intellectual knowledge, for the **wicked SHALL NOT UNDERSTAND.** How wonderfully this is true of these days. The Higher Critics have labored hard to discredit the Book of Daniel, but without avail, for the Book is more studied than ever, and is being **"unsealed"** by Holy Spirit enlightened students of the Word of God, who clearly see that we have reached the "Time of the End," and are living in the closing days of the "Times of the Gentiles."

The "unsealing" began about 100 years ago, when the **"Midnight Cry," "Behold, the Bridegroom Cometh,"** was heard in the "Revival of Premillennial Truth." For centuries while the Bridegroom tarried the Wise and Foolish virgins **"ALL slumbered and slept,"** and the Church lapsed into a condition of spiritual apathy, and "The Blessed Hope" was eclipsed. But now all over the world the Blessed Hope has emerged from the shadow, and the virgins are "trimming their lamps" preparatory to going out to meet their Lord, but only the "wise" have oil in their vessels and in their lamps. We are now living in the "Fourth Watch of the Night," soon the **"MORNING STAR"** (Christ. Rev. 22:16) will appear and we shall be caught out at the Rapture to meet Him and go into the Marriage Feast.

Let us take a hasty glance at the "Signs of the Times."

1. **POST-MILLENNIAL SCOFFERS.**

In II Pet. 3:3, 4 we read: "That there shall come in the **'Last Days' SCOFFERS,** walking after their own lusts, and saying, Where is the **promise of HIS COMING?** for since the fathers fell asleep, all things continue as they were from the beginning of the creation."

How true this is of the present day. The Doctrine of the Second Coming is "scoffed" at, and those who hold it are looked upon as deluded fanatics, and sad to say, this opposition comes from prominent religious leaders of the Day.

2. **APOSTASY.**

In II Thess. 2:3, we are told that **"THAT DAY** (the Day of the Lord) shall not come, except there come a **'FALLING AWAY'** first." This **"Falling Away"** is evidenced on every hand.

3. **FALSE TEACHERS.**

In II Peter 2:1, 2 we are warned against "False Teachers" who shall privately bring in **"damnable heresies,"** even denying the Lord that bought them, such as Christian Scientists and Russelites, and that many shall follow their **"pernicious ways,"** and sad to relate these "followers" are recruited from the orthodox church members, of whom the Apostle Paul wrote to Timothy (II Tim. 4:3, 4), saying: "The time will come when they **will not endure sound doctrine;** but after their own lusts shall they heap to themselves teachers, having **itching ears:** and they shall turn away their ears **from the truth,** and shall be turned unto **FABLES."** This "turning **away"** is evidenced on every hand. There is a "turning away" in doctrinal standards, in the demand for a regenerated church membership, in church and Sunday school attendance, and in Sabbath observance. Many church goers will not endure "sound doctrine." They will not go to hear those who preach the "total depravity" of man, the necessity of the "New Birth," and the conscious and endless torment of those who reject Christ as a personal Saviour. They demand teachers who will **"itch"** (tickle) their ears with pleasing, novel and sensational doctrines.

4. **SPIRITUALISM.**

In I Tim. 4:1 we are warned of a departure from the faith. That in the **"Latter Times"** (the Last Days of this Dispensation), some shall **"depart from the faith,** giving heed to **seducing spirits** and **doctrines of devils."** This is being fulfilled in the increasing number of those who are forsaking their Christian belief to become followers of Spiritualistic Mediums and to dabble in Psychical Research.

5. **PERILOUS TIMES.**

Of these times Paul told Timothy. "This know also, that in the **'LAST DAYS' Perilous Times** shall come. For men shall be **lovers of their own selves, covetous, boasters, proud, blasphemers, disobedient to parents, unthankful, unholy, without natural affection** (for their own offspring), **truce breakers, false accusers, incontinent, fierce, despisers of those who are good, traitors, heady, highminded, lovers of pleasures more than lovers of God:** having a **FORM of**

godliness, but denying the **POWER thereof."** II Tim. 3:1-5. We have neither time or space to enlarge upon the above, but what a catalogue we have here of the "perilous conditions" of the times in which we live.

6. **HEAPED UP TREASURE.**

In James 5:1-6, we are told that in the **"LAST DAYS"** there shall be a class of **"rich men,"** who shall have **"HEAPED treasure together,"** and that by **"FRAUD,"** and who shall use their ill-gotten gain in the pursuit of "pleasure" and "wantonness," and that God will hear the cry of those who have been cheated of their just share of the profits, and will send a sore judgment upon the guilty. What a description we have here of the unprincipled speculative and profiteering spirit of the days in which we live, when men become millionaires, and multi-millionaires, in a few years. Truly we are living in the "Last Days" of this Dispensation.

7. **A LAODICEAN CHURCH.**

In the Message to the Church of Laodicea (Rev. 3:14-22) we have a description of the last stage of the professing Church on earth. It is described as neither "hot" nor "cold," but nauseatingly lukewarm, so that Christ says He will "spue it out of His mouth." It boastingly will claim to be "rich" and "increased with goods," and to have "need of nothing," not even of Christ, for He will be excluded and will have to knock for admittance, and it will be ignorant of its true condition, that it is **wretched,** and **miserable,** and **poor,** and **blind,** and **naked.** Unspeakably sad it is that this is the condition to a large extent of the professing Church of today.

8. **THE FIG-TREE SIGN.**

When Jesus' Disciples asked Him, after He had foretold the destruction of the Temple: "Tell us, when shall these things be? and what shall be the **SIGN of THY COMING,** and of the end of the world (Age)?" (Matt. 24:1-3), Jesus gave as a "Sign" of His Coming the "Fig-Tree Sign." The "Fig-Tree" symbolizes the nation of Israel, and its "budding" the revival of Israel as a nation. Here again we have evidence of the nearness of the Lord's Return for the revival of Zionism, and the passing of the Land of Palestine into the hands of a Christian nation, opens the way for the restoration of the Jews to their own land, and the fulfillment of the Fig-Tree Sign. The fact that the City of Jerusalem surrendered without the firing of a shot is significant. Jesus said that Jerusalem was to be trodden down of the Gentiles until "The Times of the Gentiles" should be fulfilled (Luke 21:24), and the taking of Jerusalem at this time may signify that "The Times of the Gentiles" is drawing to a close.

9. **THE DISTRESS OF NATIONS.**

In Luke 21:24-27 Jesus tells us that as the "Times of the Gentiles" come to a close, "there shall be signs in the sun, and in the moon, and in the stars; and upon the **earth DISTRESS OF NATIONS,** with **perplexity;** the sea and the waves (the peoples of the earth) roaring; men's hearts **failing them for fear,** and for looking after those things which are coming on the earth: for the 'Powers of Heaven' (the Principalities and Powers of Evil, Eph. 6:11, 12), shall be shaken. And **THEN** shall they see the Son of Man coming in a cloud with power and great glory." In the prophecy of Haggai 2:6, 7, we read: "Thus saith the Lord of hosts; yet once, it is a **little while,** and I will shake the heavens, and the earth, and the sea, and the dry land; and I will **SHAKE ALL NATIONS,** and the **DESIRE** (Christ) **OF ALL NATIONS WILL COME."** This has never been fulfilled as yet, and the present **"Distress of Nations,"** the uprising of the masses in "National Revolutions," the "Tottering Thrones" and other indications that the nations are **Being Shaken,** is still further proof that we are living in the times just preceding the appearing of the Son of Man, the **"DESIRE OF ALL NATIONS"** who will bring peace to this troubled earth.

10. NOAH DAYS.

The last "sign" that we would mention is the "sign" of the "Noah Days." Luke 17:26-30. As it was in the days of Noah, they did eat, they drank, they married wives, they were given in marriage, they bought, they sold, they planted, they builded, so shall it be in the days of the Son of Man. Where you say is the sin in doing these things? They are not only commanded, they are necessary. That is true. The sin was not in "doing" them, but in doing them **"UNTIL the Flood came."** That is, they did nothing else. They forgot to worship their Maker. So today men and women are so busily engaged in doing the good things of life that they have no time to worship God. They are so busy building homes for themselves on earth that they are neglecting to secure a home in heaven. They are more anxious that their children should make a good match on earth, than that they should be united to the Lord. They are so much concerned about their case in Court, that they have forgotten that they must stand at the Judgment Bar of God. For a fuller description of these "Noah Days" see my larger work on Dispensational Truth.

11. LOT DAYS.

In the same connection with the **"Noah Days"** is classed the **"LOT DAYS."** Lot was Abraham's nephew. Gen. 12:5. The herdsmen of Abraham and Lot could not agree, and to prevent a quarrel between them, which would have been a scandal in the eyes of the heathen in whose land they dwelt, Abraham suggested a separation. Gen. 13:5-13. Lot, with the thought of worldly advantage for himself and family, first **"looked"** toward Sodom, then **"pitched his tent"** near it, then became a **"dweller in Sodom,"** and though he was a **righteous man** (not a holy man) and daily vexed his soul with the filthy conversation of the wicked (II Pet. 2:6-10), he entered into the political life of the city and became a Judge. The result was that Lot lost his **"TESTIMONY."** And when he made a plea to the Sodomites to save his **"Angel Visitors,"** and to his "Sons-in-Law" to flee, with their wives, with him, they **"MOCKED"** him. Gen. 19:1-38.

Nevertheless, because he was a child of God, though a backslidden one, he was saved **"out of Sodom."** So today there are many true Children of God who have become entangled in the world, of which Sodom is a type, and have **"lost their TESTIMONY,"** and as a result will lose the salvation of their loved ones even though they themselves, like Lot, shall be **"saved by FIRE."** I Cor. 3: 11-15. But while Lot was saved from being consumed in Sodom, Sodom could not be destroyed until Lot was taken out. So the Wrath of God cannot fall upon a wicked world until the Church is **"caught out."** II Thess. 1:7-10. There are many Lots in these days.

WAITING

There are some who would distinguish between the words **"Wait"** and **"Watch"** as applied to the "Second Coming," referring the word **"Wait"** to the "Rapture" and the word **"Watch"** to the "Revelation." While the word "Wait" is used only in connection with the "Rapture," I Cor. 1:7; I Thess. 1:10; II Thess. 3:5, the word "Watch" applies to both. The word "Waiting" is a blessed word **freighted** with **HOPE.**

1. **GOD THE FATHER** is waiting to be gracious to the Sinner.
2. **GOD THE SON** is waiting for the completion of His Bride —the Church.
3. **GOD THE HOLY SPIRIT** is waiting to escort the Bride to her Heavenly Home.
4. **THE DEAD IN CHRIST** are waiting the call of the Archangel.
5. **THE LIVING SAINTS** are waiting to be **"caught out."**
6. **THE SOULS AND SPIRITS OF THE JUST** are waiting in Paradise for their resurrection bodies.
7. **THE JEWS** are waiting for their Messiah, and restoration to their own land.
8. **CREATION** is waiting for the removal of the Curse.
9. **THE CHURCH** is waiting not for a "Love Letter" from her Beloved, not for "Precious Gifts" that will display His Riches and Bountiful Provision for her happiness, not a "Wireless Message" that will convey the thought that He, in the Person of the Holy Spirit, is with her, but she is waiting for His Personal, Bodily, and Visible Return. **Come,** Lord Jesus, **COME!**

HE SHALL COME

"What I say unto you I say unto all, Watch."
"At even, or at midnight, or at the cock-crowing."

It may be in the evening,
When the work of the day is done,
And you have time to sit in the twilight,
And to watch the sinking sun;
While the long bright day dies slowly
Over the sea,
And the hour grows quiet and holy
With thoughts of **Me**;
While you hear the village children
Passing along the street,
Among these thronging footsteps
May come the sound of **My** feet;
Therefore I tell you, watch!
By the light of the evening star,
When the room is growing dusky
As the clouds afar;
Let the door be on the latch
In your home,
For it may be through the gloaming,
I will come.

It may be in the midnight
When 'tis heavy upon the land,
And the black waves lying dumbly
Along the sand;
When the moonless night draws close
And the lights are out in the house,
When the fires burn low and red,
And the watch is ticking loudly
Beside the bed;
Though you sleep tired on your couch,
Still your heart must wake and watch
In the dark room;
For it may be that at midnight
I will come.

It may be at the cock-crow,
When the night is dying slowly
In the sky,
And the sea looks calm and holy,
Waiting for the dawn of the golden sun
Which draweth nigh;
When the mists are on the valleys, shading,
The rivers chill,
And my morning star is fading, fading
Over the hill;

Behold, I say unto you, watch!
Let the door be on the latch
In your home,
In the chill before the dawning,
Between the night and morning,
I may come.

It may be in the morning
When the sun is bright and strong,
And the dew is glittering sharply
Over the little lawn,
When the waves are laughing loudly
Along the shore,
And the little birds are singing sweetly
About the door;
With the long day's work before you
You are up with the sun,
And the neighbors come to talk a little
Of all that must be done;
But, remember, that I may be the next
To come in at the door,
To call you from your busy work,
For evermore.
As you work, your heart must watch,
For the door is on the latch
In your room,
And it may be in the morning
I will come.

So I am watching quietly
Every day,
Whenever the sun shines brightly
I rise and say,
Surely it is the shining of His face,
And look unto the gate of His high place
Beyond the sea,
For I know He is coming shortly
To summon me;
And when a shadow falls across the window
Of my room,
Where I am working my appointed task,
I lift my head to watch the door and ask
If He is come!
And the Spirit answers softly
In my home,
"Only a few more shadows,
And He will come."

—Selected.

OTHER BOOKS BY THE SAME AUTHOR

The Book of Revelation

THIS BOOK IS THE RESULT OF 25 YEARS' STUDY OF THE BOOK OF REVELATION. THE BOOK IS INTERPRETED FROM THE FUTURIST STANDPOINT. THE WRITER'S PURPOSE IS TO SHOW THAT THE BOOK IS TO BE TAKEN LITERALLY, AND THAT IT IS WRITTEN IN CHRONOLOGICAL ORDER. THE TEXT OF THE OLD VERSION IS USED, AND IS PRINTED AT THE TOP OF EACH SUBJECT. THE TEXT AND DESCRIPTIVE MATTER IS EMPHASIZED BY THE USE OF CAPITALS AND BLACK TYPE.

The book is illustrated with over 30 charts, maps, and diagrams. There are also numerous cuts of the symbols, beasts, etc., spoken of in the Book of Revelation, distributed through the book. These help to elucidate the text and add to the value of the book, and save much explanatory matter. The make-up and printing of the book is unique. The divisons and headings of the subjects are all printed in heavy black type. This adds to the cost of the book, but makes the subject matter of the book stand out in bold relief. While there are but 225 pages in the book, the size of the type, and the enlarged page, 6x9 inches, make it equivalent to an ordinary book of 400 pages.

The book is sane, contains no speculative matter, nor opinions of the writer. The book is not a commentary made up of quotations from other writers. The writer is neither a copyist or compiler. The only **Author** the writer has sought to follow is the Author of the book, the **LORD JESUS CHRIST.** He has simply sought to interpret the **"MIND OF CHRIST"** as revealed in the Book of Revelation. The writer's aim has been to prepare a standard work on the Book of Revelation, from the Futurist Standpoint, that can be used as a text-book in Theological Seminaries and Bible Schools, and a help to Ministers, Missionaries, and Bible Students, generally. Its appearance at this time is timely, when the prophetic utterances of the Book of Revelation are rapidly approaching their fulfilment.

The Spirit World

THIS BOOK GIVES THE TEACHINGS OF THE HOLY SCRIPTURES AS TO THE "SPIRIT WORD." IT CONTAINS 19 CHAPTERS, AND IS ILLUSTRATED WITH 27 PICTURES AND 17 CHARTS.

It treats of the "Powers of Good and Evil," of the "Underworld," of "Satan," of the "Fallen Angels," of "Demonism," of "Soul Sleep," the "Intermediate State," the "Resurrections" and "Judgments" and of "Heaven" and "Hell."